SALLY'S GONE, SHE LEFT HER NAME

Russell Davis

BROADWAY PLAY PUBLISHING INC
224 E 62nd St, NY, NY 10065
www.broadwayplaypub.com
info@broadwayplaypub.com

SALLY'S GONE, SHE LEFT HER NAME
© Copyright 2003 by Russell Davis

This play was originally published by B P P I in March 2003 in a collection entitled *Plays by Russell Davis*.

1st printing: Dec 2008. 2nd printing: Sept 2010.
I S B N: 978-0-88145-391-1

Book design: Marie Donovan
Word processing: Microsoft Word
Typographic controls: Ventura Publisher
Typeface: Palatino
Printed and bound in the U S A

SALLY'S GONE, SHE LEFT HER NAME was produced at People's Light & Theater Company, Malvern, PA, opening on 28 April 1999. The cast and creative contributors were:

SALLY	Elizabeth Webster
HENRY	David Strathairn
CHRISTOPHER	Mark Del Guzzo
CYNTHIA	Joyce Cohen
Director	Abigail Adams
Scenic designer	James F Pyne, Jr
Lighting designer	Thomas C Hase
Costume designer	Marla J Jurglanis
Production stage manager	Charles T Brastow

There were earlier productions at The Academy Theater, Atlanta (16 February-18 March 1989); New York Theater Workshop, N Y C (23 April-26 May 1985), American Stage Festival, Milford, NH (17-28 July 1984); Center Stage, Baltimore (20 March-26 April 1981).

There were readings and development work at New Dramatists, N Y C; The Road Company, Johnson City, TN; George Street Playhouse, NJ; Harold Clurman Theatre, N Y C; Saint Nicholas Theater, Chicago.

An earlier version of this play was published by *Plays in Process*, Theatre Communications Group, N Y C, June, 1985.

CHARACTERS & SETTING

SALLY, *a teenager*
HENRY, *her father*
CHRISTOPHER, *her younger brother*
CYNTHIA, *her mother*

A kitchen. There is a table with four chairs. Above the table hangs a lamp. Surrounding this table and chairs is a very solid-looking kitchen. It has walls, windows, cabinets, utensils, and appliances. There are three entrances into this kitchen: from the front hall; from the back hall and backstairs; and from the backdoor to the garage and the lawn outside in back. Through the windows of this kitchen, and behind the walls, we see an empty horizon. As if all the rest of the world has been removed.

Time: summer

ACT ONE

Scene One

(SALLY *sits alone at the end of the table. She wears a white nightgown. It is night. Enter* HENRY *through the backdoor. He carries a briefcase. Pause)*

HENRY: Sally. Sally, you're up. (*Comes into the kitchen. He puts his briefcase down.*) You sitting around, or something, Sally? What are you doing up?

(SALLY *shrugs her shoulders.*)

HENRY: *(Gently)* Well, come on, then. It's late. Why don't you go on up? Get yourself back to bed.

(SALLY *stands. She goes to the backstairs.*)

HENRY: What is it, Sally? Something wrong?

(SALLY *stops.*)

HENRY: You can't sleep?

SALLY: No.

HENRY: How come?

SALLY: Just can't.

HENRY: Okay. Is there something we could talk about? Would you like to stay down here and talk?

SALLY: I don't know.

HENRY: Come on. Would it help if we just sat and talked?

SALLY: I guess.

HENRY: Fine. Then let's talk. Let's have a little meeting right here. At the table. In the middle of the night.

SALLY: It's not the middle.

HENRY: Well, it's one o'clock. So what is it, Sally? We should talk about? What do you think about up there in your room when you can't sleep? And it's one o'clock? I bet you think all kinds of things.
     You think about Bruce?

SALLY: No.

HENRY: How come? What's the matter with thinking about Bruce?

SALLY: I just don't think about him.

HENRY: Does he know this?

SALLY: What?

HENRY: You're not thinking about him anymore.

SALLY: I don't have to think about Bruce.

HENRY: Okay. You think about Mom?

SALLY: What about Mom?

HENRY: Well, how was she?

SALLY: She's okay.

HENRY: She had a good day today?

SALLY: I think so.

HENRY: Yes. I thought so too. We spoke on the phone. (Pause) It's kind of dark in here. How about if we turn on another light?

SALLY: Don't, Dad.

HENRY: You don't want more light?

SALLY: I like it like this. Nighttime.

HENRY: Okay. (*Goes to the refrigerator. He opens it.*)
Would you like some chocolate milk?

SALLY: Hm?

HENRY: I'm in the mood for chocolate milk. Or ice
cream. Which would you like, chocolate milk, or ice
cream?

SALLY: I don't want anything.

HENRY: Come on. It'll help us talk.

SALLY: No, thank you.

HENRY: Okay. (*Takes chocolate milk out of the refrigerator*)
So. Is it college? You nervous about going to college?
I am.

SALLY: I don't think so.

HENRY: Well, what is it, Sally? What is it we can sit up,
the whole night, talk about? What's on your mind?
What thoughts?

SALLY: I can't tell you any thoughts. I don't know them.

HENRY: You don't know your thoughts?

SALLY: I just can't sleep.

HENRY: I never heard of that. Not knowing thoughts.
What else can you know, except your thoughts?

SALLY: Dad, I used to know what I thought.

HENRY: I know. You've told me lots of times.

SALLY: I just don't anymore.

HENRY: What do you mean, you don't anymore?

SALLY: I can't tell what I really think.

HENRY: About what, Sally?

SALLY: Everything. It's everything I think.

HENRY: Okay. And it's not your mother, then?

SALLY: It's everything, Dad, I told you. I'm sorry.

(Pause)

HENRY: Fine. I guess I wouldn't sleep either.
  Maybe it's just a spell. Some sort of spell, that's all.
Somebody snuck in here and cast a spell. Spooked our
whole house. So we don't know now what to think.
Any one of us. *(Pause)* I don't know. You used to tell me
things. I remember. All kinds of problems. And I would
find an answer. Hear these magic thoughts in my head.
The right things to say. I remember how good that felt.
Having the right thing to say. To help you out. *(Picks up
his briefcase)* Well. You're older now. Pretty much an
adult. Off to college. You want to be left alone, I know.
I think I'll go upstairs now. Leave you alone.

SALLY: I'll be okay alone, Dad.

HENRY: I know. *(Regards the kitchen)* You know. I look at
this kitchen sometimes. The whole house. I find myself
looking at it. Can't quite seem to see it the way I used
to. I feel something's been moved. Some book I put
down. Or note. I wrote a note once to myself. Which
I can't find. I get that feeling in this house.
  I've taken to bumping into walls, for example.
Particularly upstairs in the hall. I bump into the wall
like I'm surprised it's there. I'm not sure it always was.
I have trouble in the dining room too. Or the front hall.
I feel like it's my body. My body has these extra added
parts, or pieces, to it, which I can't quite see, except
I feel too big now for this house. Or maybe everything
shifted two inches. And I never noticed. I bump walls,
or into the door, because it's moved from where it was
before. Some invisible two inches.
  Whereas at work I don't notice these things. What's
invisible. My body feels fine. I feel fine in my office
at work. I know what each person does and what I do.
Where the walls are. I feel totally focused. Until it's time
to come home. And slowly, but surely, I lose focus each

evening I'm home in this house. *(Pause)* It's just a phase, Sally. That's all. Your lack of sleep.
My problem sometimes with focus.
It's important to think of these things sometimes as phases. Not what's real. What's real is you and me, Sally. Our family. Mom and Chris. It's real we live together, right here, in this house. This is our home. Even if something should happen and all the rest of the world were gone. Everything ended. The end of time. This is where we should be.
And all these other thoughts, what makes us uneasy, restless, that's all just a phase. *(Pause)* You're smiling.

SALLY: Uh huh. Yes, Dad.

HENRY: What did I say? To make you smile.

SALLY: Just thinking, that's all. If you yelled.

HENRY: Really? Yelled what?

SALLY: If it's the end of the world out there, Dad. The end of time. And you yell at Mom and Chris and me. To get back into the house. *(Pause)* You want some more chocolate milk, Dad?

HENRY: Hm?

SALLY: I'm going to have chocolate milk.

HENRY: Sure. Bring some more. I'd like that.

(SALLY goes to the refrigerator.)

SALLY: Tomorrow's Saturday.
You staying home Saturday?

HENRY: Yes. I am.

SALLY: Okay.
You going to take Chris bowling, then? Christopher wants to go bowling. He's pretty sure, Dad, he can beat you now.

HENRY: He's going to beat me?

SALLY: That's what he says. At bowling.

HENRY: Fine. I'll be sure to take him bowling.

(SALLY *pours chocolate milk.*)

SALLY: How was your trip, Dad?

HENRY: It was fine.

SALLY: Was it important?

HENRY: What, the trip?

SALLY: Sure. What's it like to take a plane? And go someplace for just a day?

HENRY: It's just business, Sally. People doing business. Buying property. Making plans.

(SALLY *brings chocolate milk to the table.*)

SALLY: You're away a lot, Dad. Makes me worry.

HENRY: I know.

SALLY: What if something happened?

HENRY: Why? What's going to happen?

SALLY: I don't know. You could lose touch.

HENRY: Sally, I'm not going to lose touch. I'm just working. These things gather their own steam, that's all. I'm sorry. It'll pass. Be calm again.

(*They drink chocolate milk.*)

SALLY: How's Brigid?

HENRY: Hm?

SALLY: You working with Brigid?

HENRY: Yes, I am.

SALLY: She ever go with you?

HENRY: What, to travel?

SALLY: Yes.

HENRY: No, I haven't asked her.

SALLY: Uh huh.

HENRY: Sally. You don't seem to like Brigid.

SALLY: She's okay.

HENRY: She works very hard. I appreciate that.

SALLY: I think she likes you, Dad.

HENRY: What?

SALLY: That's all.

HENRY: Brigid Porto likes me?

SALLY: Uh huh. I believe so.

HENRY: What do you mean, she likes me? I should hope so. That she likes me. And if she doesn't, she should keep it to herself.

SALLY: She's attracted to you, Dad.

HENRY: Brigid Porto?

SALLY: Yes.

HENRY: But that's ridiculous, Sally. I'm old enough to be her father.

SALLY: You are not.

HENRY: Sally, I'm really old enough.

SALLY: She's over thirty, Dad.

HENRY: Over thirty?

SALLY: She told me. Last time I visited you.

HENRY: Wow. I thought she was younger. I was sure she was younger.

SALLY: She's been married, even.

HENRY: What?

SALLY: Your new associate, Dad. You didn't know that?

HENRY: No. No, I guess I didn't remember.

SALLY: Yep. Married. Before she even came to this country.

HENRY: Really? Well, I'm sorry she had to go through that. A divorce. Especially in Brazil.

SALLY: Yeah. She said it's hard.

HENRY: I didn't realize you spent so much time talking with her.

SALLY: I can talk, Dad.

HENRY: Good.

SALLY: I just think she likes helping you.

HENRY: But that's her job, Sally. Helping me. That's why she was hired. And as far as her personal feelings, about being such help, that doesn't actually have to concern me. It's important she help. She's tremendously smart. At what she does.

SALLY: Okay. I understand.

HENRY: Anyway, I'm sorry, I am. If that's what's keeping you up. Being away so much like this. It'll pass, I'm sure. All that stuff out there, my work, it fluctuates. *(Pause)* Anything else, then, Sally? That's keeping you up?

SALLY: I can't paint.

HENRY: Hm?

SALLY: It's painting, Dad. That's all.

HENRY: What do you mean, you can't paint?

SALLY: You think you might be glad?

HENRY: What?

SALLY: If I can't paint anymore? I might be happier now? In a regular college?

HENRY: Come on, Sally. What is this?

SALLY: I'm just telling thoughts.

HENRY: Sally, your college has an art department. A very good one.

SALLY: Maybe I don't want to paint anymore.

HENRY: Fine. Then let's talk about this, okay? Why you're not painting. Is it because of art school? You're not going to New York or Paris? I'm not letting you go like that?

SALLY: No.

HENRY: You sure? This isn't some kind of intense renunciation? A nasty sublimation...

SALLY: I don't care which college I go to.

HENRY: ...all because of your father?

SALLY: No, Dad. I just can't paint. I'm stuck.

HENRY: You're stuck? On what?

SALLY: I've never, ever, been so stuck. Ever. On the same spot. Over and over. I'm stuck.

HENRY: Sally.

SALLY: It's making me scared. How stuck I can be. How I can't leave this spot. I feel crazy. I want to smash this spot. Want to force it.

(Pause)

HENRY: Is this what you're working on upstairs?

SALLY: Yes.

HENRY: I'm sorry, Sally. About your painting. Just try a different picture, I don't know, that's all. Move to another spot.

SALLY: I don't want to try a different picture.

HENRY: No?

SALLY: No. I'm stuck on this one. *(Pause)* Whereas
it used to be simple, Dad. It was simple making
mountains and trees. Painting rivers. A little stream
to go through the woods. With ripples and leaves.
Sunlight. I could paint like that forever. Paint oceans
and beaches. Birds in the sky and all kinds of cows
in a meadow.

(Lights focus on SALLY.)

SALLY: Because that's my ideal. What I believe in. To
paint what's in the world, what's all around, learn to
paint like that. Be realistic. Like Grandpa. Before I get
to haul off, presume to be some kind of diverse, abstract
painter like everybody's supposed to be. Because it's
mean spirited, I think, how we're expected to paint.
Lose touch with what's kind, or generous, what's
common to all. What might be compassionate.

But all of a sudden that doesn't count anymore.
This ideal. What I thought. Because I'm stuck now
on a house. I can't get past the bottom windows.
Above the lawn. I can't get them connected with a
window upstairs. One window. With sky reflected in it.
They don't connect. I can't get the rest of some house
to put these windows in. I have empty space instead. A
gap in between. With no way across. In which all colors
are wrong. Nothing fits. I have to scrape it away. Over
and over. The same spot. And it's making me mad.
Upset. Because how can I have windows like that with
no house to be in? How can it be all divided like this?

And now I'm starting to think abstract. Is there some
surreal way to connect these windows? But everything
feels phony. When I try to fill this gap. This colorless
crack right through the middle of my painting which
I cannot cross. Nothing is real. I can't make it real.
Like I want to wash it away. Make rain come and wind,
a big flood wash away this house.

And so I decided, finally, I don't know how to do this.
How'm I going to think of myself, ever, as a painter?
If I can't even paint this house?
  My very own home.

(Blackout)

Scene Two

*(The kitchen, as before. Except the wall behind the
refrigerator and stove has been removed. Some cabinets are
gone too. We can now see a framed oil painting hanging in
the air behind. As if it were on a front hall wall. It is the
painting of someone running along an ocean beach at night.
HENRY is at the table, having a sandwich, going through a
folder of papers. It is late the next morning. CHRISTOPHER's
head appears at the back hall entrance. He looks into the
kitchen. He regards HENRY at the table. CHRISTOPHER's
head disappears. Pause. CHRISTOPHER appears at the
entrance to the front hall. He regards HENRY. He disappears
again. Pause. Enter CHRISTOPHER from the back hall.)*

CHRISTOPHER: Hi, Dad.

HENRY: Chris. Hi.

CHRISTOPHER: Your trip okay?

HENRY: Hm?

CHRISTOPHER: You have a good trip yesterday?

HENRY: Yes, I did. Thank you.

CHRISTOPHER: You making money, Dad? Same as usual?

HENRY: I guess. *(He continues going through papers.)*

*(CHRISTOPHER goes to the refrigerator. He winks at no one
in particular. He opens the refrigerator.)*

CHRISTOPHER: I've been meaning to tell you, Dad.
I think you better watch out. Yeah. Because someday

soon I'm going to catch up. Pass you by. Uh huh.
In bowling. Probably ping pong too. I figure you got
maybe a month left, that's all. So you better enjoy this,
Dad, your last month, beating me bowling and ping
pong. Cause I already passed Sally long ago.
 I warned her too.
 Which is all just a sign, Dad. A premonition. Of the
wonders to come. Because I think someday you're
going to be shocked. Uh huh. At how easy it's going
to be for me to pass you by even making money.
Just warning. Because I'm going into entertainment.
Yep. That's the field I'm going to be in. Entertainment.

HENRY: Chris. What are you eating?

CHRISTOPHER: Me?

HENRY: Yes.

CHRISTOPHER: Cheese.

HENRY: Cheese, huh? Would you have some bread,
please, with that cheese?

CHRISTOPHER: Yes, Dad. (*Goes to the bread drawer.
He takes out bread. He makes faces.*)

(HENRY *goes through his papers.*)

CHRISTOPHER: I can tell you're not taking it seriously.
My warnings.

HENRY: No, I listen, Chris. I listen.

CHRISTOPHER: Okay. (*Takes more cheese from the
refrigerator. He puts it in his sandwich. He opens the
backdoor to the lawn. He exits. He enters. He winks.
He closes the backdoor. He goes to the refrigerator.*)

CHRISTOPHER: Where's Mom?

HENRY: Upstairs, I believe.

CHRISTOPHER: Is she coming down?

HENRY: Sure. Doesn't your mother always come down?

CHRISTOPHER: Yeah, sure. She comes down.

HENRY: She's trying to get some reading done.

CHRISTOPHER: Yeah? What's Mom read these days?

HENRY: She's trying some psychology books.

CHRISTOPHER: Really? Psychology.

HENRY: Trying to understand herself, yes.

CHRISTOPHER: Uh huh. Psychology books good for that, Dad? To understand yourself in?

HENRY: Some of them, sure.

CHRISTOPHER: Uh huh. Mom say anything? About these books.

HENRY: No. Not yet.

CHRISTOPHER: You think she might?

HENRY: Well, sure. But, Chris, your mother doesn't really talk. About what she's reading. These library books about fables and poems. I mean, I can ask. And sometimes she really surprises me. How she can suddenly talk. And I sit there and listen to all this stuff, these deep things, I guess, she's been thinking about.
   But mostly she's quiet about it. I don't like to disturb her. She seems to need quiet. *(Pause)* Would you close the refrigerator door, Chris?

CHRISTOPHER: Huh?

HENRY: There's no need to leave the door open like that.

CHRISTOPHER: Sure, Dad. *(Closes the refrigerator)*

(HENRY returns to his papers. CHRISTOPHER opens the backdoor. He closes it. He winks. HENRY regards him.)

HENRY: Chris. You make more fuss about being in a room than anyone I know. Why can't you, for once, just simply stay put? Be still.

CHRISTOPHER: Cause I'm thinking, Dad.

HENRY: Thinking? What's thinking got to do with playing with the door in here?

CHRISTOPHER: Come on, Dad. I'm thinking about the entertainment field.

HENRY: The entertainment field?

CHRISTOPHER: Dad, coming into a room, how you do that, is important in the entertainment field.

HENRY: Oh.

CHRISTOPHER: Sorry, Dad. I got to practice these things.

HENRY: Fine. Then would you take your practice someplace else?

CHRISTOPHER: Hm?

HENRY: I said, Practice in another room, Chris. It's a big house. I'd like to get a little work done here.

CHRISTOPHER: Sure, Dad.

HENRY: And when you come into a room, it would be nice, for once, if you could calm down. Respect whoever's already here.

CHRISTOPHER: I'm calm, Dad. Very calm.

HENRY: No, you're restless.

CHRISTOPHER: Restless? Come on, Dad. I'm just excited. If you were thinking about what I think, you'd be excited too.

HENRY: Well, good. I'm glad it's exciting for you. I am. Just leave the backdoor alone in here.

(HENRY *returns to his papers.* CHRISTOPHER *goes to the refrigerator.*)

CHRISTOPHER: Sally's painting our house, Dad. Did you know that?

HENRY: Hm?

CHRISTOPHER: Sally. She has this painting of our house. Up in her room.

HENRY: Uh huh.

CHRISTOPHER: Weird, Dad. How she's painting the house. I think you should probably talk to her.

HENRY: Talk to Sally about our house?

CHRISTOPHER: Uh huh. It's weird.

HENRY: What is?

CHRISTOPHER: It looks like some kind of lightning went and struck our house. Split it right down the middle.

HENRY: The house?

CHRISTOPHER: Yes, Dad.

HENRY: How do you even know it's our house? What she's painting.

CHRISTOPHER: Because it's the same house. I can tell.

HENRY: But it's a painting.

CHRISTOPHER: No, it's got the same shutters, same colors, chimney, except split in two. Like a giant saw came and sawed our house. Some monster ate through the middle and now there's nothing left. Just the path through the house which the monster took. On top of which you should see how she's chewed up the lawn. It's got potholes. Or bomb craters. Big holes a bear could live in, I swear, right in the middle of the lawn. This is your lawn, Dad. Half of which didn't get mowed. It's long enough for some serpent to glide around in. Or a jungle to start growing. And you should see what she's done to your lawnmower. It's like the end of the world. Like you changed the oil a hundred years ago. Or it got found on the bottom of an ocean. Come on, Dad. You should go up and take a look at this. Really. Before she takes it any further.

(HENRY *stands. He closes the refrigerator door.*)

HENRY: The refrigerator, Chris?

CHRISTOPHER: Huh?

HENRY: I've told you, Chris. About this refrigerator door.

CHRISTOPHER: Yes, Dad.

HENRY: You should also eat at the table.

CHRISTOPHER: Right, Dad.

(CHRISTOPHER *goes to the table. He sits.*)

HENRY: What were you doing, Chris? In Sally's room?

CHRISTOPHER: I can look in Sally's room.

HENRY: No, I'm sure she didn't ask you in to look at what she's painting.

CHRISTOPHER: I can't look, Dad? If the door was open?

HENRY: I doubt it, come on. Sally doesn't leave her door open.

CHRISTOPHER: No, I've seen it open. Lots of times.

HENRY: You don't open it, Chris? You don't sneak in?

CHRISTOPHER: No, I do not open Sally's door.

HENRY: Then why are you talking to me about this? Why don't you talk to Sally?

CHRISTOPHER: I do talk.

HENRY: Tell her what you think.

CHRISTOPHER: She doesn't listen. She's my sister.

HENRY: Oh? You think she'll listen to me?

CHRISTOPHER: Yeah. I sure hope so.

HENRY: Why?

CHRISTOPHER: Because it's getting out of hand, Dad.
It's weird. We're supposed to stand around and do
nothing? Just watch my own sister go weird?

(Pause)

HENRY: Chris. I think Sally can paint our house any
way she pleases. That's her business. What she does
in her room is her business.

CHRISTOPHER: Yeah? Well, it's not your business?
If your own daughter goes weird?

HENRY: Sally's not weird.

CHRISTOPHER: No, Dad, Sally does lots of things now
you probably wouldn't approve.

HENRY: Come on, Chris. I'm not going to bother Sally
about a painting.

CHRISTOPHER: Okay, Bruce, then. She's weird with
Bruce.

HENRY: What is?

CHRISTOPHER: She's calling him up, Dad, sometimes
in the middle of the night. I hear her.

HENRY: Chris, what are you doing up in the middle
of the night?

CHRISTOPHER: I can't help it, Dad, if I go to the
bathroom. If I look out the window and there's Sally
outside. Sitting on the lawn. Or she's on the phone.
Leaving long messages on Bruce's machine how she
can't sleep. If he doesn't wake up and talk, she'll never
sleep.

HENRY: Sally does that?

CHRISTOPHER: Yeah. I heard her.

HENRY: Maybe, then, I should talk to Sally.

CHRISTOPHER: You better, Dad. Cause it's getting real hard to sleep around here.

(Pause)

HENRY: Fine, Chris. I'll talk to her.

CHRISTOPHER: Thanks, Dad.

HENRY: I'll ask.

CHRISTOPHER: Sure. Cause I miss the old days with Sally, I do. When I used to look up to her. I could walk right in, Dad. To her room. We didn't used to close our doors. I could tell Sally my plans. What I'm going to do in life. And she used to draw faces for me. Any face I asked. She talked about painting too. What's in this world. It made me proud. How Sally was going to paint the world. It's not like that anymore, Dad. It's all gone secret. Whatever Sally thinks about, it's a secret now.

HENRY: She's getting ready for college, Chris. That's all, come on. She may not feel she can talk to you so much.

CHRISTOPHER: Mom, too, Dad.

HENRY: What?

CHRISTOPHER: Mom's gone secret.

HENRY: Chris, your mother's always been a secret.

CHRISTOPHER: Not to me, she wasn't.

HENRY: No, you're just older now.

CHRISTOPHER: Come on, Dad. You know she's more secret.

HENRY: Fine. So let her be secret, Chris. People don't always have to talk. It gets easy, Chris, when you're older, to run out of words. Your mother's run out of words, that's all. Stories to tell. She's recharging, right? It's just a phase. It's not what's real about your mother. What's real is how great she's been over the years. And this whole thing, the hospital, these sessions now with a doctor, that's just a phase.

And you're her son. You've got to help your mother by understanding that. That it's just a phase.

Okay? That's your responsibility.

CHRISTOPHER: Yes, Dad.

HENRY: Good.

Meanwhile I'll ask Sally about Bruce. Okay? And I'll ask her questions too, about her painting.

CHRISTOPHER: Okay.

HENRY: Whatever these secrets you feel, Chris, I'm sure it's all just a phase.

CHRISTOPHER: Yeah. Yeah, I think so too.

HENRY: Good, then.

(HENRY *stands at the window.*)

CHRISTOPHER: You thinking about the lawn, Dad?

HENRY: Hm?

CHRISTOPHER: You going to mow the lawn?

HENRY: Yes. Yes, I think I'll go do that. Take care of the lawn. How about you?

CHRISTOPHER: I'll go fix my room.

HENRY: Good.

CHRISTOPHER: Then Mom's going to take me away to soccer practice.

HENRY: That's good.

CHRISTOPHER: Fine, Dad.

(Exit CHRISTOPHER *up the backstairs.* HENRY *continues to look out the window. Enter* CYNTHIA *from the front hall. She looks at the wall that's gone from behind the stove and refrigerator.* HENRY *turns from the window. He sees* CYNTHIA.*)*

HENRY: Cynthia?

(No response)

HENRY: Cynthia. Have you had anything to eat?

*(*CYNTHIA *looks away from the empty wall.)*

HENRY: May I get you something, Cynthia?

CYNTHIA: Henry?

HENRY: Yes?

CYNTHIA: I'm worried, Henry. About Sally.

HENRY: Really?

CYNTHIA: Yes. She's still upstairs in bed.

HENRY: No, I know. She was up very late last night. Insomnia, I think. We talked about it. She was up when I came in. I'm not sure when it was she finally went to bed.
   I'll go and wake her soon.

*(*CYNTHIA *goes to the refrigerator. She opens it.)*

HENRY: How was your reading this morning?

CYNTHIA: I don't like it.

HENRY: No?

CYNTHIA: What I'm reading, no.

HENRY: Why? What's it say?

CYNTHIA: I'm not sure it's always so helpful. To suggest these things.

HENRY: What things?

CYNTHIA: Well, I don't know, Henry. That we're interfered with in some way.

HENRY: Really?

CYNTHIA: Well, as children, yes. Or by society.

HENRY: Hmm.

(CYNTHIA *brings a glass of milk to the table.*)

HENRY: Well, that's what they all say now, don't they? These books.

CYNTHIA: Yes. I think they do.

HENRY: And you've read that kind of stuff before?

CYNTHIA: Yes, I have.

HENRY: It's probably what your doctor talks about too, isn't it?

CYNTHIA: Hm?

HENRY: The psychiatrist, Cynthia. The one you see. Ian Heisel.

CYNTHIA: We talk, yes.

HENRY: Right. So what bothers you particularly now? About this stuff.

CYNTHIA: I'm just afraid, Henry. Don't you get afraid sometimes?

HENRY: Of what?

CYNTHIA: All these suggestions.

HENRY: What particular suggestions make you afraid?

CYNTHIA: There's nothing particular, Henry. I just remember if you found yourself thinking about something, and it wasn't good to think about, you tried to stop yourself thinking about it.

HENRY: Yes, I remember.

CYNTHIA: It feels more helpless.

HENRY: What is?

CYNTHIA: There're all these reasons now. To be helpless.

HENRY: Right.

CYNTHIA: You told me just this week about your elevator man. At the office.

HENRY: Yes, I know.

CYNTHIA: That man killed his girlfriend. You told me. And then himself. And this was a man whom everyone liked. You said he was special.

HENRY: Yes.

CYNTHIA: So where did he get this idea he had to do those things?

HENRY: He obviously became obsessed.

CYNTHIA: With what?

HENRY: This woman, Cynthia. His girlfriend.

CYNTHIA: But he was a good man. You said so.

HENRY: I know.

CYNTHIA: So how could a good man go and do that?

HENRY: I don't know.

CYNTHIA: I don't either. *(Pause)* I think he may have read too much.

HENRY: Read what, Cynthia?

CYNTHIA: Some of those newspapers, Henry.

HENRY: Yes?

CYNTHIA: Yes, the ones that talk about these things. What can happen. All the time.

(Pause)

HENRY: I agree, Cynthia. I do. Seems to me when I first came into this world, people had stray thoughts. That's how they were classified. A stray thought. That's all. Some idea, or notion, that passed through your mind from somewhere out there in the universe. Like a neutrino. It passed through your head and on through the earth below and then back out there into deep space. And like a neutrino, rarely would a stray thought actually bump into anything substantial, rarely could it become an actual visible fact. It was just a thought that occurred to you on its way to nowhere. Like in college. Like why don't I stand up on this table in the middle of this class and pee on all my books? That is basically a stray thought. It speaks of nothing essential about myself. Or if I was with my father, for example, and I think, why don't I slam this car door on all my father's fingers? So he won't think anymore he can paint. And he can go out instead and earn some real money. Get a job. That is a stray thought. It does not mean it's supposed to happen. *(Pause)* For example, you and I, Cynthia. We began as a thought. That's all. Just some thought which I very quickly dismissed. Because I saw the men who wanted to be with you in this college. How they had cars. Were all white. They took trips on weekends. I heard them invite you. Ask you out to ski.

Whereas I worked at a diner. I walked back to my dorm, every day, down a dirt road behind the college. Until I saw you once on a horse. Two guys also with you on horses. The three of you coming my way. And I thought, this woman is so quiet. Each time I see her. I've never seen a person quiet like this. And as I stepped aside to let your horses pass, I could hear these guys make clever chitchat. But what I noticed was your eyes. That they looked at me. You quietly watched me. And as I walked on I had this thought, I should ask her out. I think I should do that. Ask her out.

Which of course was ridiculous. I could never do that.

And when we did actually go out, I was shocked.
Grateful. We were kept a secret. Until your parents
came. They found out. My father was a poor painter,
a failed artist. And my mother, she wasn't even white.
So they forbade you. You had to listen. Which was the
biggest crisis of my life. Because I found myself having
these thoughts. All these stray, inappropriate ideas.
I found myself waiting in hallways, or some corner,
in case you would pass. Found myself repeatedly going
back to the place we would meet. The little stream you
had taken me so we could be out of sight. A clump of
trees with a meadow nearby. I kept going to those trees,
hoping to see you there, that you would come back too,
just to remember and I would see you.

And I think I teetered there. Almost lost it. All desire
to study, make something of my life. I became focused
on you. Vulnerable to any passing thought. And I think
only one thing saved me.

Which was I was embarrassed by my thoughts.
Lurking around after you. This was my terrible secret.
Because I was a man, Cynthia. That's what helped me.
The dumb idea I was a man. And a man is not like this.
A man does not grow up needing like this.

And so I stopped. Fought hard and I stopped. Got to
the point where I could say, Damn, that was something.
The way that woman just rode in like that, and out of
my life again.

And then three years later it started all over again.
Except you were ready now. To leave your parents.

And I was ready too.

But what if it hadn't swung that way? If I hadn't
thought it so abnormal? Something to reject. A guy
behaving like this? What if I had thought myself maybe
justified? If I read about other guys, strong and nice
like me, going to pieces too?

Am I really so very different, then? From the guy
in my building? Who killed his girlfriend, and then

himself? *(Pause)* I'm sorry, Cynthia. I've been thinking about this. All week. *(Pause)* You were talking about Sally. Your concern for Sally.

(Pause)

CYNTHIA: Henry. You never told me that.

HENRY: What?

CYNTHIA: How you used to go to that stream. The stream where we sat.

HENRY: No, I know.

CYNTHIA: Why not?

HENRY: Because it frightened me.

CYNTHIA: What did?

HENRY: Being there by myself. It frightened me.

CYNTHIA: But we went back. We've been back.

HENRY: No, Cynthia. I could never tell you how close we came to never getting married.

CYNTHIA: But I know how close.

HENRY: No, you couldn't know. Not this.

CYNTHIA: But I do know, Henry. You think I married you because you had some sort of focus. Because you knew what you wanted in this world. And everybody else I knew was effete, pampered.

HENRY: Well, no, Cynthia.

CYNTHIA: No, that's what you said. But maybe, Henry, I didn't marry you at all for what you think. All this focus you think, what you think you could do in the world. Maybe I married you because I knew you had been frightened, even if you never said so, I knew how frightened. And I loved you, Henry, because I saw you come back from that. You came back from being frightened.

And I wanted to be with a man like that. Who could come back like that from being frightened.

(HENRY *goes to* CYNTHIA. *He takes her hand. He kisses her. They sit together at the table.*)

HENRY: Cynthia. You used to tell me something.

CYNTHIA: What was that?

HENRY: About being real. Remember you used to tell me?

CYNTHIA: I wasn't real?

HENRY: That's right. That's what you told me.

CYNTHIA: Yes.

HENRY: I thought that was amazing.

CYNTHIA: What was?

HENRY: That someone could feel like that. Not real.

CYNTHIA: No, Henry.

HENRY: Well, but I was young, Cynthia. That kind of thought had never occurred to me. That I wasn't real.

CYNTHIA: I'm sorry.

HENRY: No, come on. It made it very special.

CYNTHIA: What was special?

HENRY: When we used to sit together like that, Cynthia. By that stream. And you told me, quietly, how you weren't sure if you were real. And I said, Yes. You are realer to me than all this world. And I swore right then I would make you feel it too. How real.

(CYNTHIA *smiles. She puts her head on* HENRY's *shoulder.*)

HENRY: I think we should go somewhere, Cynthia. Someplace quiet, don't you think?

CYNTHIA: Hm?

HENRY: Take a vacation. A vacation together, just you and I. Get you away from that doctor. All those books. We should travel.

CYNTHIA: You'd like to travel?

HENRY: Well, sure.

CYNTHIA: Where, Henry?

HENRY: I don't know. Where would you like?

CYNTHIA: I can't think.

HENRY: What about Switzerland?

CYNTHIA: Switzerland?

HENRY: Yes. Should we go there, to Switzerland?

CYNTHIA: Why, what's in Switzerland?

HENRY: Well, you like winter.

CYNTHIA: Yes?

HENRY: Winter must be especially nice, right, in Switzerland? All those mountains. The snow.

CYNTHIA: Yes, I think so.

HENRY: So maybe we should go there. Plan on it together. Sally'll be in college, and Chris'll be fine at friends'. And we could plan on that. On Switzerland. Would you let me do that, Cynthia? Take you to Switzerland?

CYNTHIA: Yes, Henry.

HENRY: Thank you.

CYNTHIA: Of course you could take me.

HENRY: Good. *(Pause)* Well. Maybe I should go get Sally. Wake her up. Get that daughter of ours up.

(HENRY *stands.*)

CYNTHIA: Henry?

HENRY: Yes?

CYNTHIA: Sally was outside last night.

HENRY: Outside, huh?

CYNTHIA: After you came in, yes.

HENRY: Okay.

CYNTHIA: She was sitting out there on the lawn.

HENRY: Really?

(CYNTHIA *stands.*)

CYNTHIA: Yes, Henry, I got up to go to the window.
To look at the moon in our window. But I saw there
was snow on our lawn. This patch of snow. Until I
realized, no, that's Sally. In her white nightgown. She's
sitting out there in the moonlight. Staring at our house.
　　And then she got up. Went across the lawn and down
the street. And I thought, how can Sally do that? Walk
down our street in the nightgown she likes to wear to
bed?
　　So I went downstairs. I saw your father's painting in
the front hall was gone. And the kitchen light was on.
I came in here and your father's picture, the ocean at
night, was right here, against this chair. Sally must have
been looking at it. So I went to the living room to wait
for Sally, but I must have fallen asleep, Henry. Because
when I got up your father's painting was back in the
hall. And the kitchen light was out. I went upstairs to
Sally's room. To ask her about going down the street
like that. Ask about Bruce. Tell her some stranger
could drive by, someone we don't know from another
neighborhood, or passing through, could see her
dressed like that in the middle of the night.
　　But her door was closed and her light was out. So I

listened. And I opened that door. But Sally was asleep.
She was fast asleep.

(Lights focus on CYNTHIA.*)*

CYNTHIA: And so I went back to bed. Lay down in bed.
And then I saw I was actually lying on a hill. Way
above the ocean. And I thought, what am I doing above
the ocean? On a hill? So I sat up to look around. And
just below me I saw trees. I heard the sound of water.
Some stream. And I thought, good. It must be morning.
So I got up to walk down to the stream. I thought I
should wash my face and hands in this stream. And
as I walked I thought, it is so lovely here. In this land.
It feels so real. I wonder what land this is. Where have
I seen this land before?

And so I came to the stream, which was actually now
as big as a river. And I saw there was a house across
a field. I could hear people and sounds inside. I didn't
know if I should go in and say hello. If I should ask
where I was. But then I saw there was a dirt road I
should take just beneath the trees. I could see this road
going away far into the distance. And I remember
hoping, please, God, don't let my head explode again.
If I should take this road.

Then someone came out of the house, I think, to say
something to me. They called out. But I just waved.
Waved to them.

And as I took the road, I felt happy, thinking, I'm
going to visit Sally. I will finally get to visit with my
daughter. And as I looked down at my feet, I noticed
I was wearing Sally's shoes. Her bright, red, buckled
shoes. And I was wearing her nightgown. This simple
white gown. Which began to billow in the wind.

And then I heard my voice. A happy voice saying,
Goodbye.

And it was Sally's.

My voice was Sally's.

(Blackout)

Scene Three

(The kitchen, as before. Except part of the wall near the front hall entrance has now been removed. The oil painting hanging in the air behind the kitchen is much larger. Too big, in fact, to fit in the front hall. It is of an adolescent girl running along an ocean beach at night.)

(CHRISTOPHER sits alone at one end of the table. He eats a piece of cheese. The refrigerator door is open. It is two weeks later. Late at night. Enter SALLY through the backdoor. Pause)

SALLY: Chris.

Chris, you're up. *(Pause)* What are you doing like this, up?

(CHRISTOPHER continues to eat his cheese. SALLY closes the refrigerator door.)

SALLY: Chris. You know how Dad feels about electricity. *(Sits at the other end of the table)*

CHRISTOPHER: How's Bruce?

SALLY: Hm?

CHRISTOPHER: Your date with Bruce.

(No response)

CHRISTOPHER: Did he explain yet how come he's going out with you?

(No response)

CHRISTOPHER: I've been waiting for an explanation.

SALLY: Don't, Chris. Please.

CHRISTOPHER: Hm?

SALLY: I can't banter now.

CHRISTOPHER: No?

SALLY: Not now, no.

CHRISTOPHER: What's the point of a sister if she can't banter?

SALLY: I just can't.

CHRISTOPHER: Why, Sally? Bruce knock all the banter out of you?

(No response. CHRISTOPHER *stands. He regards the painting in the front hall. He crosses to the backdoor. He opens it. He closes it.)*

CHRISTOPHER: I heard Dad talking to Mom yesterday. You know what Dad says? He thinks maybe they should change the painting in the hall. Get rid of Grandpa's picture of the ocean. Dad doesn't like walking past that picture all the time. Doesn't like where it is. He says it's right in the center of our house. Like we all have to walk around it.
   He thinks we could use something else.
   Besides he thought the picture would go better in your room. You'd like it up there with you.

(Pause)

SALLY: Where's Mom?

CHRISTOPHER: Upstairs. In bed.

SALLY: Asleep?

CHRISTOPHER: Sure, she's asleep.

SALLY: Okay. How come you're up?

CHRISTOPHER: I got hungry.

SALLY: It's the middle of the night.

CHRISTOPHER: It's not the middle.

SALLY: Pretty close.

CHRISTOPHER: It's one o'clock.

SALLY: That's the middle around here.

CHRISTOPHER: The middle for you too. You're supposed to be in, Sally. You're not supposed to be out late like this with Bruce.

SALLY: Well. Dad isn't back.

CHRISTOPHER: He isn't?

SALLY: No. His car isn't back. I just looked.

CHRISTOPHER: So? Then Dad's still working.

SALLY: Working, huh?

CHRISTOPHER: Working, yeah, Sally.

SALLY: Okay.

CHRISTOPHER: Yeah. That's what Dad does. He works. How do you think we get to live here, Sally? In this house?

SALLY: Come on, Chris.

CHRISTOPHER: No, we live here because Dad works. Unlike Grandpa out there who didn't work. Didn't get a job. Dad's work built this house. This place we get to live. Where we can each have our own room. Our own door to close. Whereas Dad had nothing. No door for himself. He had to grow up together in the same room, the living room, with Aunt Ruth. That's why Dad works. Why he's out. So he can give to us in this house what nobody gave to him. *(Pause)* Sally? Are you crying?

(No response)

CHRISTOPHER: Ah, Sally.

SALLY: It's nothing, Chris.

CHRISTOPHER: Hm?

SALLY: No, just me and Bruce. That's all.

CHRISTOPHER: What's you and Bruce? Why you're crying?

SALLY: I'm not crying. Come on.

CHRISTOPHER: No, then who's crying?

SALLY: It's not me, crying.

CHRISTOPHER: No? There's a second Sally in here crying?

SALLY: Come on, Chris. I told you. I told you I can't banter like this anymore.

(Pause)

CHRISTOPHER: Okay. That's okay, Sally. If you need to be private. I can understand.
   Seems to me, however, it didn't used to be so private around here. Something way too private's going on. Feels secret. It's all gone secret now. Spooky. And it's not just Mom. What's secret about Mom. *(Regards the kitchen)* I don't know. Dad says it's a phase. It's all just a phase. Nothing real. What we're going through.

(Pause)

SALLY: There's no secret, Chris. You shouldn't have that idea, something secret. I see no secret. No big secret anyone should tell.

CHRISTOPHER: Uh huh. Then how come it feels weird. In this house.

SALLY: What?

CHRISTOPHER: Come on. You don't notice anything?

SALLY: No, Chris. It's not weird.

CHRISTOPHER: Seems just normal?

SALLY: I think so. Normal, sure.

CHRISTOPHER: Uh huh. How come you took that walk?

SALLY: What walk?

CHRISTOPHER: Two weeks ago, your walk. In the middle of the night.

SALLY: I take walks, Chris. I told Dad. I can't think anymore in this house. I have to get outside, away from here. What's the big deal? It's just me taking a walk. I'm not allowed to go out and think?

CHRISTOPHER: In a nightgown, Sally?

SALLY: I'm supposed to dress up for a walk?

CHRISTOPHER: No, what if somebody looks out their window?

SALLY: Well, I'm sorry.

CHRISTOPHER: They're going to think they saw a ghost, or something. Or what if there's a robber?

SALLY: Chris. We don't have robbers.

CHRISTOPHER: You don't know what could happen here at night.

SALLY: I'm telling you, Chris. I saw no robbers.

CHRISTOPHER: Well, no, it's weird, I'm sorry. If you can't think anymore in this house. It's your own house, Sally. Where're you supposed to think?

(Pause)

SALLY: Look, Chris. Maybe we should go upstairs. It's time, I think, for bed. *(Gently)* Come on, Chris. What if Dad comes back soon and we're still not in bed?
  Come, Chris. Let's go upstairs. *(Starts for the backstairs)*

CHRISTOPHER: Well. That's another thing, Sally. I hate to mention.

SALLY: What's that?

CHRISTOPHER: Your painting. What you're painting up there.

SALLY: You saw my painting?

CHRISTOPHER: Come on. I've been quiet about it too long.

SALLY: You saw that painting?

CHRISTOPHER: Yeah. What you're doing in your room.

SALLY: It's none of your business what I paint in my room. It's not even finished.

CHRISTOPHER: Then how come you leave your door open?

SALLY: I did not. I did not leave it open.

CHRISTOPHER: You did so, Sally. It was right there, open.

SALLY: I still didn't invite you in. You have no business going into my room like that, all the way into my room, to look at what I'm painting.

CHRISTOPHER: Why? Because it's weird?

SALLY: What?

CHRISTOPHER: Your painting is weird. You shouldn't make our house look so weird.

SALLY: It's not our house.

CHRISTOPHER: Yes, it is so our house. Don't try to tell me what's our house.

SALLY: Chris, it's not our house. It's something different. It's mental.

CHRISTOPHER: Oh, yeah? It's not our house? It's mental? Then how come it's got the same shutters and roof, all the lawn outside? Except distorted.

SALLY: Because it's mental, Chris. It's not the house.

CHRISTOPHER: It is so. You're painting it like somebody exploded. We had an explosion in this house.

SALLY: There's no explosion. Come on.

CHRISTOPHER: Then why's the house split like that in two?

SALLY: Why should you care anyway how I paint a house?

CHRISTOPHER: Because it's where we live. Our house. What you're painting upstairs. You're painting it flying apart. Painting Mom's face lost in a window upstairs. Like she's not even here anymore. You got her face up there with the clouds and all the sky reflected in the window. And that lawn, Sally. It looks blasted. Like Mom took off, with the whole top half of our house, and everything left behind is blasted and empty looking. You have no business taking what happened to Mom, putting it like that in a picture.

(Pause)

SALLY: *(Stunned)* That's what you see in my picture? Mom taking off?

(No response)

SALLY: I'm not trying to take, Chris, what happened to Mom. And put it in any picture.
  I'm just trying to paint a house.
  It's just a picture, Chris. It's not even finished.

(CHRISTOPHER *opens the refrigerator.*)

CHRISTOPHER: You have a responsibility now, Sally. Dad said so.

SALLY: What responsibility?

CHRISTOPHER: Ever since Mom got hurt we have a responsibility.

SALLY: What? I shouldn't paint anymore? Because of Mom?

CHRISTOPHER: What if Mom should see that picture?

SALLY: Mom?

CHRISTOPHER: Yeah, if she saw.

SALLY: Mom doesn't sneak into my room, Chris, like you.

CHRISTOPHER: She'll still see it.

SALLY: It's not even finished. What's the big deal?

CHRISTOPHER: I can see you understand nothing about Mom.

SALLY: What?

CHRISTOPHER: Anything about protecting Mom.

SALLY: Oh? So you're the expert now, huh? On Mom? *(She slams the refrigerator door shut.)* Chris. If you can't be rational at this hour, we have no business being up. Talking about Mom. 'Cause Mom could look and not see what you're talking about. Some face lost in a window. This explosion which I didn't paint. No. I painted two parts of a house which can't fit together, okay, Chris? It's just a gap. Right where I can't finish. That's why there's a gap. Because I'm stuck. Stuck on a spot. I didn't finish up there what you had no business taking a look at.

(Pause)

CHRISTOPHER: You should grow up, Sally, you should. Accept responsibility around here again. Instead of trying to float off somewhere. In your thoughts. In the middle of the night, like in your nightgown. Like you're some floaty girl Grandpa painted. Some girl running off.
  Because I used to count on you. On what you thought. But you don't care anymore what I count on. Or what

Dad asked. How he asked us to be responsible now for Mom around here. *(Opens the refrigerator. He looks inside.)*

SALLY: Dad asked us to be responsible? Because of Mom?

CHRISTOPHER: That's right. He did.

SALLY: And Dad himself is responsible, you think?

CHRISTOPHER: Of course Dad's responsible.

SALLY: About Mom?

CHRISTOPHER: Sure, Dad cares all the time what happens to Mom.

SALLY: Uh huh. Then where's Dad?

CHRISTOPHER: Where's Dad?

SALLY: Yeah, Christopher. Why isn't Dad upstairs right now? Why isn't Dad back in bed?

CHRISTOPHER: Because he's working. I told you. He took a trip.

SALLY: Close the refrigerator door, Christopher.

CHRISTOPHER: You close it.

SALLY: What?

CHRISTOPHER: You close it yourself, this door, if you think it's so important.

SALLY: I thought you believed in Dad.

CHRISTOPHER: I do believe.

SALLY: Then close the door. That's what Dad believes. You should close the door.

CHRISTOPHER: I'm eating.

SALLY: You should eat over there at the table. Even if it's the middle of the night.

CHRISTOPHER: *(Tossing a piece of cheese into the refrigerator)* Keep it up, Sally, okay?

SALLY: Christopher, get that cheese out of there.

CHRISTOPHER: What cheese?

SALLY: You took a bite out of that cheese. Cut that bite off.

CHRISTOPHER: This cheese?

SALLY: Yes. Get that cheese out.

CHRISTOPHER: This cheese is my cheese.

SALLY: You're lucky, dammit, Dad isn't here.

CHRISTOPHER: Yeah, well, somebody's got to work around here. Unlike Grandpa.

SALLY: He's not working, Chris! So stop saying he's working!

CHRISTOPHER: Get out of here, Sally!

SALLY: No, he is not! He is not! Bruce and I just saw him not working! *(She pulls the cheese out of the refrigerator. She throws it across the room.)* We saw him, Christopher! Dad! At the airport! He came in at the airport. From his trip. I was there! To surprise him. Make him happy. Like the old days, I was going to meet Dad. But there was someone else. Somebody there first. At the airport, waiting to meet Dad, surprise him. And I warned Dad about this person. I did. I warned she liked him. Warned him right here. And I saw Dad was surprised. To see her there, waiting for him. And then all of a sudden he was glad. Like he couldn't stand it any longer how glad he could be. That's how come I know Dad's not upstairs. How his car isn't back. Because he's out right now with someone else. Visiting with her, right now, at her house.

(Pause)

CHRISTOPHER: You and Bruce saw Dad?

(Pause. SALLY picks up the piece of cheese. She puts it on the table.)

SALLY: I'm sorry, Christopher.
   You shouldn't keep saying that about Dad. Or Grandpa. About work. I'm sorry.

(CHRISTOPHER closes the refrigerator door.)

CHRISTOPHER: You know this person? At the airport?

SALLY: Yes. I've met her.

CHRISTOPHER: Where?

SALLY: When I visit Dad at work.

CHRISTOPHER: She works?

SALLY: Yes, with Dad. She works in his office.

CHRISTOPHER: Uh huh.

SALLY: I hate her.

CHRISTOPHER: What?

SALLY: I hate this person, Chris.

(Pause)

CHRISTOPHER: Is she pretty? Does this mean she's pretty?

(Pause)

SALLY: Mom's prettier.

CHRISTOPHER: Yes?

SALLY: Yes.

CHRISTOPHER: A lot prettier? Or just a little?

SALLY: I think a lot.

CHRISTOPHER: Maybe she's smarter. Maybe Dad decided to talk to someone smarter.

SALLY: Chris. Mom's smart.

CHRISTOPHER: Not like she used to. Mom used to talk.

SALLY: Chris, Mom talks. She just doesn't speak up, that's all. Maybe it hurts. But she's still smart. Mom will always be smart.

CHRISTOPHER: She used to leave messages.

SALLY: What?

CHRISTOPHER: There were messages once. Telling us what to do.

SALLY: Yeah. Yeah, there were.

CHRISTOPHER: Errands on the refrigerator, yeah. Or in the bathroom.

SALLY: Things to think about, yes.

CHRISTOPHER: Notes on my bed,

SALLY: Lots of little pieces of paper, I know.

CHRISTOPHER: I miss when Mom did that.

SALLY: I do too. *(Pause)* I miss Mom coming too into my room at night. Telling us about Dad. How she met Dad. And what her parents thought. *(Pause)* I miss Mom's stories too. What she made up. About that little girl. Who had a moat. She saw a moat all around her. Between her and the rest of the world. Her own body even. Like she was locked up by herself, all alone in her mind. There was nothing she could do to cross that moat. Nobody to rescue her. And when she became a woman, no man on earth, no prince of this world, could win her. The more they tried, the deeper her moat.
    Until she decided to go off in the middle of the night. Sneak away from her land. Go to the end of the earth. When the earth was still flat. And rest herself, sit on the edge of the earth, maybe drop off. Disappear. And nobody would know, or be to blame. But on her

way she ran out of roads. And saw what looked like a
sleeping beast. Between her and the edge of the earth.
And just as she was about to sneak around, this beast
woke and grabbed her. Began to shriek. Each time the
beast shrieked, a piece of the earth broke off until she
was about to fall herself. But someone must have
caught her. Because she woke up. In an enchanted
forest. And in this forest she could see there was no
moat. *(Pause)* Ragatelle. I loved to hear about Ragatelle.
Who saw a moat. Mom's stories about the sleeping
beast. Ragatelle's adventures in a forest. The wizard she
met. How Ragatelle never had to go back to the land
she came from. Where she could see that moat. *(Pause)*
I think when we were all in that car and Mom got hurt,
I don't think it's because Mom banged her head like
that against the car door. Whereas the rest of us were
fine. Just walked away. I don't think some door which
closed on her put Mom in a coma. No. Because I
remember coming to the hospital, thinking how can
Mom's body, or what she thinks, be so flimsy? How
could Mom leave us alone like this? Why is it my mom
who has to see some sleeping beast? My mom who
hears this shriek? How can I ever possibly understand,
how can it be explained now, what I might have to
someday see myself at the end of this world? *(Pause)*
Oh, I know Mom's out of the hospital now. Sees a
doctor. Has therapy. But I don't think they know what's
up with Mom. How to put her back. I think Doctor
Heisel just likes her. He calls. Misses her when she
doesn't make an appointment. But he doesn't know
about Mom. How she looks ahead. How she can see
right past. What feels so solid to all the rest of us.

(Sound of a car. SALLY *and* CHRISTOPHER *go to a window.)*

SALLY: It's Dad. I can't meet Dad.

CHRISTOPHER: He's looking, Sally.

SALLY: I know he's looking.

CHRISTOPHER: He can see right at us.

SALLY: I can't meet him anyway.

CHRISTOPHER: He can see from the garage.

SALLY: I don't care what Dad can see. I'm getting out of here. *(She exits up the backstairs.)*

(CHRISTOPHER almost follows her. Instead, he opens the refrigerator door. He remembers his piece of cheese. He retrieves it from the table.)

(Enter HENRY through the backdoor.)

HENRY: Chris.

CHRISTOPHER: Hi, Dad.

HENRY: What are you doing, Chris?

CHRISTOPHER: Hm?

HENRY: What are you doing up?

CHRISTOPHER: I'm hungry.

HENRY: Uh huh.

CHRISTOPHER: I woke up hungry.

HENRY: What about Sally?

CHRISTOPHER: Sally?

HENRY: Yes. I just saw Sally.

CHRISTOPHER: Oh. Sally can't sleep.

HENRY: No?

CHRISTOPHER: She's been talking about her lack of sleep.

HENRY: I'm sorry. Did she just get in?

CHRISTOPHER: Nah. She's been here talking.

HENRY: Okay.

CHRISTOPHER: Bruce let her out early.

HENRY: Chris, would you mind closing the refrigerator door?

CHRISTOPHER: Hm?

HENRY: The refrigerator, Chris.

CHRISTOPHER: Sure, Dad. *(Closes the refrigerator)*

HENRY: Why don't you get on up to bed?

CHRISTOPHER: We were just talking about Mom, Dad.

HENRY: Hm?

CHRISTOPHER: That's all.

HENRY: You were talking about Mom?

CHRISTOPHER: Yeah. Yeah, we decided Mom's gone kind of quiet.

HENRY: You decided?

CHRISTOPHER: Yeah, quiet. Kind of changed.

HENRY: I think your mother's always been quiet.

CHRISTOPHER: Yeah.

HENRY: As long as I've known her.

CHRISTOPHER: Well. She's silent now.

HENRY: Huh?

CHRISTOPHER: Kind of silent.

(Pause)

HENRY: I think I'll have some ice cream.

CHRISTOPHER: Yeah?

HENRY: Yes. I really need some ice cream.

CHRISTOPHER: Me, too, Dad.

HENRY: You want ice cream?

CHRISTOPHER: Sure.

HENRY: Okay. We'll have some ice cream. *(Takes a box of ice cream out of the refrigerator. He puts it on the table.)*

HENRY: Chris?

CHRISTOPHER: Yes, Dad?

HENRY: Chris, your mother used to tell me she never felt real. That's what I remember.

CHRISTOPHER: Uh huh.

HENRY: She couldn't feel real. Chris, when you find your first woman, make sure she feels real.

CHRISTOPHER: Yeah?

HENRY: Yes. Yes, I think a man sometimes wants a woman like that. Who's otherworldly. Because the world's not nice out there, Chris. In the office. It's manipulative and unfair, and I want something otherworldly. Innocent to come home to. *(Pause)* I've been in love with your mother for a long time now. *(Looks blankly at the kitchen)*

CHRISTOPHER: You need help, Dad?

HENRY: Help?

CHRISTOPHER: You need a spoon, or something, for the ice cream? Bowls?

HENRY: Yes. Yes, some bowls.

CHRISTOPHER: Or do you want to forget about it?

HENRY: Forget the ice cream?

CHRISTOPHER: Yeah.

(They look at the ice cream on the table.)

HENRY: Yes, I think so. I think we can forget the ice cream. Do you mind?

CHRISTOPHER: No, Dad.

(HENRY picks up the box of ice cream.)

HENRY: Anyway, Chris. Your mother's quiet because she still doesn't feel real. After all these years.
I haven't made her real. *(He returns the ice cream to the freezer.)*

CHRISTOPHER: Dad?

HENRY: Hm?

CHRISTOPHER: Dad, that's okay. About Mom.

HENRY: What is?

CHRISTOPHER: Lots of time I don't feel real either. It's just a phase, Dad. Remember?

HENRY: A phase?

CHRISTOPHER: Yeah, you told us what's real, Dad. It's our family. Nothing else at all has to be real.

HENRY: Chris?

CHRISTOPHER: Anything else is just a phase, that's all, Dad. I promise you. Only a phase.

(Lights focus on CHRISTOPHER.)

CHRISTOPHER: Cause I have them, Dad, myself. Lots of phases. And Sally, you see her. She's worse than the moon. How she sits out there on our lawn. In the middle of the night. When I get up to go to the bathroom. The first time I thought she was a sheet. I thought, that's weird. Who could have left that white sheet out there on our lawn? And then I thought, is that a dead body? It's a body, I bet, under that sheet. Who could have left that sheet over a dead body on our lawn? Until I realized, no. No, wait, that's Sally. That's my sister out there. In her white nightgown. I wonder should I go out and talk to her?
But I decided to get back to bed. Get some sleep. But just as I was lying down I noticed I had an arrow in my chest. Somebody outside must have shot an arrow. Which came through my window and landed

right where I was in bed. So I got up to go to the bathroom again to take this arrow out. Except I heard Dad downstairs in the kitchen. Talking to some people outside, telling them not to come in. But when I went downstairs, I could see nobody he was talking to. Then Dad asked what was wrong, and I told him about the arrow which somebody shot in my chest. But he couldn't see it, any arrow which came through my window.

So I went to my room to get the arrow, but by then I saw my whole bed had arrows, sticking up on it, all over. I decided I better close this window. Except the wall was gone. The whole wall to our house. And I was standing on the edge of my room holding just the window. And while I held the window, I saw that white sheet again. Caught up there in a tree. Flapping in the wind. And then I saw at my feet there was a ditch, which had water. Which then got deeper and wider. Like a moat. And I saw the sheet in the tree across the water get further and further away from me, accelerating, until it became like a star in the night.

And I was standing there, looking at this star, when I heard somebody call out behind me. They called, Goodbye.

(The stage darkens. HENRY *is gone.)*

CHRISTOPHER: But when I looked back, I saw our house was gone. The whole house. I couldn't tell anymore it was ever there. *(Pause)* Mom? *(Pause)* Mom? Is that you? Did you call, Mom, goodbye?
Was that you?

(Blackout)

END OF ACT ONE

ACT TWO

Scene One

(The kitchen, as before. Except the whole front hall wall is gone, as well as the wall behind the refrigerator and stove.)

(The backdoor and part of that wall is gone too. The oil painting hanging in the air behind now reaches above the kitchen. It is as large as one of the missing walls. The figure in the painting, the adolescent girl running along an ocean beach at night, is life-size. CYNTHIA *sits at one end of the table. She looks at the missing wall beside her. It is very early the next morning. Enter* SALLY *from the lawn outside.)*

SALLY: Mom. You got up, huh?
  It's only you and me, Mom, down here? Chris and Dad still in bed?

(No response)

SALLY: I bought you something, Mom. You want to see what I went out and bought?

*(*CYNTHIA *looks away from the missing wall.)*

SALLY: I walked, Mom. Just now into town. Took an early morning walk. The stationery store was the only place open. So I went in, just to turn around from my walk. But I saw these animals. All these tiny creatures on a shelf in back. *(Puts a paper bag down on the table)* You want to see, Mom? What I bought for you? See? Right in this bag, animals. Magnetic creatures. For putting notes on the refrigerator. Things to remember on the bathroom cabinet. See, here's a lion, Mom. A lioness too. I bought a cow, look, and a bull. A lamb. Couple of tigers. Birds, fish. Two of everything, Mom, I had to buy them all. I think somebody around here, a local potter, made these ceramic creatures, and painted them, put these magnets on the back.

(CYNTHIA *looks at the creatures on the table. She picks one up.)*

SALLY: That's a dove, Mom. Look how nicely made it is. It's flying. Doesn't it make you want to write a note? Some note again to put with that dove? *(Pause)* Mom? Can you hear?

CYNTHIA: Hm?

SALLY: Can you hear me?

CYNTHIA: I hear.

SALLY: What?

CYNTHIA: I said, I hear.

SALLY: Okay.

CYNTHIA: You're talking about creatures.

SALLY: Hm?

CYNTHIA: All these creatures you bought.

SALLY: That's right. What I got this morning.

CYNTHIA: What can we do with these?

SALLY: What?

CYNTHIA: I didn't know you had so much money.

SALLY: Mom, you got to learn to project your words. I can barely hear what you're asking.

CYNTHIA: I said, These must have been very expensive.

SALLY: Well, it's pottery, Mom. I charged them.

CYNTHIA: Yes?

SALLY: Yep. All these creatures.

CYNTHIA: You charged who?

SALLY: Well, Dad.

CYNTHIA: He knows?

SALLY: What?

CYNTHIA: Does Dad know?

SALLY: Mom, some mornings, I swear, nobody can hear you. You have to speak up.

CYNTHIA: I speak up.

SALLY: You're a mother. You got to learn to speak up.

CYNTHIA: Perhaps you don't listen.

SALLY: I listen. I can barely hear. It's like you talk to yourself. You murmur.

CYNTHIA: I didn't murmur.

SALLY: Might as well. Whereas before, Mom, at least we could hear.

CYNTHIA: Maybe there was something to say.

SALLY: What?

CYNTHIA: I don't think, Sally, your father will be pleased. With these creatures you charged.

SALLY: Mom. We can figure that out later. About Dad.

CYNTHIA: Couldn't you just buy two, or three?

SALLY: No, Mom. I wanted them all. I want you to use them. Cover this whole house with notes. Write those notes again.

CYNTHIA: What notes, Sally?

SALLY: The notes. What you used to write Chris and me. What to watch out for each day. What to remember. I want you to write that down again, all the little warnings you gave. Write them for Dad too. *(Opens a drawer. She takes out a pencil and pad of paper. She comes back to the table.)* Come on, Mom. Let's write a note for Chris. Right now. So when he wakes up, he'll see there's a note. Waiting for him in the bathroom. It'll make him happy, I know. To see you writing messages again. Keeping us posted, each day, on what to do.

(CYNTHIA regards the pad and pencil.)

SALLY: Can you think of something? Huh? For Christopher?

CYNTHIA: Yes?

SALLY: Good.

CYNTHIA: I don't know where to start.

SALLY: Hm?

CYNTHIA: How to start.

SALLY: Okay. Let's start with you love him.

CYNTHIA: I love him?

SALLY: Uh huh. You have to start with that.

CYNTHIA: Okay.

SALLY: Write it down. You love him.

CYNTHIA: *(Writing)* I love you.

SALLY: Good. Now you can write about the refrigerator.

CYNTHIA: The refrigerator?

SALLY: Yes. Tell him to sit from now on at the table, Like everybody else. Write that down, where Chris must eat. At the table.

CYNTHIA: *(Writing)* Eat at the table.

SALLY: Good. And we need another note, Mom.
Chris bites the cheese in there and puts it back.

CYNTHIA: Bites?

SALLY: Yes, Mom, and we've got to do something
about the way he pretends. What he makes up.
Write that down, go on.

CYNTHIA: Write what, Sally?

SALLY: Come on, how he makes faces and talks to
himself. He comes into a room. Winks at invisible
friends. He's too old, Mom, to have friends like that,
winking friends. He's fourteen.

CYNTHIA: Yes.

SALLY: It's not cute anymore.

CYNTHIA: *(Writing)* Chris is fourteen.

SALLY: Good. That's good.
    And I want a note too, Mom.

CYNTHIA: Hm?

SALLY: Yes, write me something. What I should do.

CYNTHIA: Oh, I don't know, Sally.

SALLY: Yes, you can. You can think up a note.

CYNTHIA: About what?

SALLY: I don't know. Tell me about Bruce.

CYNTHIA: Bruce?

SALLY: Yes. If I should stay with Bruce.

CYNTHIA: You're going to college.

SALLY: I know. But Bruce wants to visit there, Mom.
I need some kind of note, I do, about Bruce.

CYNTHIA: I'm sorry.

SALLY: How come I'm going out with Bruce. A guy like that. I want somebody to talk about painting. Look around at the world outside. Have ideas. Things to say. Not somebody hanging out all the time. Being popular. Mom, I'm just wasting time, I am. Ever since Dad said I had to go to Swarthmore, I can't go somewhere like New York, Mom, I've just been hanging out. Forgetting what I used to want. I wanted to paint. You should tell me to shape up. You should write a note. I think you've had enough time since the hospital, I do, to write such a note. At least about Bruce. Maybe not to call him anymore. Don't answer his calls. Or some other note, Mom, it doesn't matter, at least something to focus my attention on this summer before I go off to college.

(*Pause*)

CYNTHIA: All right, Sally. I'll write you a note.

SALLY: You will?

CYNTHIA: Yes. I promise.

SALLY: Good. Okay, good. And what about Dad? We need to write something for him too.

CYNTHIA: We do?

SALLY: Oh, yes, Mom.

CYNTHIA: Why? What should we write?

SALLY: Well, I don't know. We could start, I guess, for example, with Grandpa's picture.

CYNTHIA: In the hall?

SALLY: Yes. Leave a note about that. 'Cause I heard Dad suggested taking it down. He doesn't want Grandpa's picture of the ocean anymore. Thinks we have to walk around it, or something. Like it's in the middle of our house.

CYNTHIA: Yes, I know.

SALLY: And we don't want that, do we? Dad taking Grandpa's ocean from our house?

CYNTHIA: No. No, we don't.

SALLY: No, 'cause it's a good picture. Grandpa painted it.

CYNTHIA: I like it, yes. Very much.

SALLY: Good. So write down for Dad to keep his hands off Grandpa's picture.

CYNTHIA: *(Writing)* Keep hands off hallway picture.

SALLY: Because it's a great picture to have, Mom, in the middle of our house, it is.

CYNTHIA: *(Writing)* Let it stay where it is.

SALLY: That's good. Can we put it up?

CYNTHIA: Hm?

SALLY: Let's put it up right now. The note to Dad. On the refrigerator, okay? *(She takes* CYNTHIA's *note and two refrigerator magnets. She places them on the refrigerator.)* Yep. I think Dad's going to see it here. Get the message, all right. About Grandpa's picture. *(She comes back to the table.)*

*(*CYNTHIA *looks at the missing wall beside her.)*

SALLY: I talked to Aunt Ruth last night, Mom. I couldn't sleep at all. So I called her.
You know what she told me. What Ruth said, Mom, about Dad? Ruth told me Dad helped Grandma move Grandpa out of his room.

CYNTHIA: Hm?

SALLY: The studio room Grandpa used.

CYNTHIA: He's dead.

SALLY: What?

CYNTHIA: Grandpa's dead.

SALLY: When Dad got back from college, first vacation, they moved Grandpa out. So Dad could have his own bedroom. Not share the living room like that with Ruth.

CYNTHIA: Sally, I think Ruth distorts.

SALLY: What?

CYNTHIA: She distorts.

SALLY: Come on, she's Dad's sister. She grew up with him.

CYNTHIA: You should talk to your father. Not just Ruth.

SALLY: Dad's just jealous. Mom, Ruth lives in New York. She does what she wants in life. She does. Ruth is a photographer.

CYNTHIA: I thought she was a waitress.

SALLY: What?

CYNTHIA: Ruth is a waitress, Sally.

SALLY: So, Mom? She has to be a waitress. She can at least talk to me about Dad. How they grew up. How Dad helped move Grandpa. So Grandpa couldn't paint anymore. In his own house.

(CYNTHIA *looks at the missing walls.* SALLY *regards her.*)

SALLY: Mom?
   Mom, you look so young sometimes. So quiet. Like a picture from somewhere.

CYNTHIA: I'm not quiet.

SALLY: What do you think about there, Mom? What is it makes you so quiet?

CYNTHIA: Sally, please. It's nothing, really. What I'm thinking.

SALLY: Well, I don't know, Mom. I keep wishing I could behave more like you. Be so quiet. Instead of blurting out all the time what's on my mind.

CYNTHIA: You don't blurt.

SALLY: Sure feels like it. Like blurting. *(Pause)* You remember Ragatelle?
The girl. With an invisible moat all around her.

CYNTHIA: Yes. I do.

SALLY: Do you miss telling those stories to us? About Ragatelle?

CYNTHIA: I miss it, yes.

SALLY: I could have listened to one last night, Mom.

CYNTHIA: Yes?

SALLY: Uh huh. I could have. I couldn't sleep.

CYNTHIA: You should have woken me.

SALLY: Woke you?

CYNTHIA: Yes. I would get up.

SALLY: No, Mom. I can't.

CYNTHIA: Why not?

SALLY: Because you're in there with Dad. I can't wake Dad.

CYNTHIA: Sally.

SALLY: No, come on, Mom. I'm not waking Dad. *(Pause)* Mom, I'm sorry. I get restless. In this house. I do. I don't know how you can stay so quiet like this. I just feel like blurting. I don't want to turn out this way. What we are in this house. This way of thinking. This is not the way we should be, you and I, in the world. All comfortable. While Dad gives shelter. No, I get restless thinking like that. Mom, I do. I want something more. I want what

Grandpa had. What made him poor. I want how he painted.

(Lights focus on SALLY.)

SALLY: Like that girl.

I want to be the girl Grandpa painted.

More than anything I know I want to be like that picture. Something like that picture.

Then I'd get to wear that wide headband she's got around her head. And that white gown that's so light you can see the nighttime through it. It floats. Like a veil.

I want to run out like that in the middle of the night. To the ocean, more than anything I know. Far away from any town, or teachers, family, or house. Just run up and down. Yes. Visit the mountains and hills. Wander the wilderness. Hear my voice cry. Clap my hands and sing. Because I think if I could do that, be some kind of little girl spirit all over again, do that and not miss all the stuff, everything in my life, the people, things to do, then I would be happy. Happy in a way for sixty years or so until I die. Go off to some other world. Wearing nothing but this same white gown and a headband. Except on my head I've embroidered: "Sally's gone."

That's right. Sally's gone.

And she left her name, so don't try calling after her. She's left her name.

(The sound of the ocean)

(Blackout)

Scene Two

(The kitchen. A last section of wall remains standing near the back hall entrance. The oil painting of the ocean now takes up almost the whole stage beyond the kitchen. Except we no longer see the adolescent girl. HENRY *is reading the note on the refrigerator. It is later that morning.* CYNTHIA *appears at the back hall entrance. Pause)*

HENRY: Cynthia?
   Is this from you? A note here on the refrigerator.

*(*CYNTHIA *comes into the kitchen.)*

HENRY: *(Reading)* "Henry. Keep your hands off the hallway picture. Let it stay where it is." *(He takes the note off the refrigerator. He looks at the refrigerator magnets.)* Where did these come from? This lion and bear?

CYNTHIA: Sally bought them.

HENRY: Really? They look expensive.

CYNTHIA: Yes.

HENRY: Very pricey knickknacks. Artistic. *(Opens the refrigerator. He closes it.)* I'm sorry I slept late.
   Chris, too. He's sleeping late. *(Comes to the table)*

CYNTHIA: Would you like something, Henry?

HENRY: Hm?

CYNTHIA: For breakfast?

HENRY: No. Thank you, Cynthia. I think we should go out.

CYNTHIA: Hm?

HENRY: Let's go out and get breakfast. Can I take you, please, out for breakfast?

CYNTHIA: Yes, thank you. Henry.

HENRY: Good, Cynthia.

(CYNTHIA *looks at the remaining wall standing near the back hall entrance.*)

HENRY: Did you speak, by the way? With Doctor Heisel?

CYNTHIA: Hm?

HENRY: Ian Heisel. He called here last week, remember? About your appointment.

CYNTHIA: Oh, yes.

HENRY: You didn't speak, then?

CYNTHIA: No. No, I'm sorry.

HENRY: Okay.
   Have you stopped seeing him, Cynthia, or something? Doctor Heisel?

CYNTHIA: Yes. Yes, I have.

HENRY: Oh. Is that wise?

CYNTHIA: Wise? I think so. I think it's wise.

HENRY: Why is that?

CYNTHIA: I'm not sure it helps anymore, Henry. Seeing Doctor Heisel.

HENRY: Okay. Then why are we still paying for this?

CYNTHIA: We're paying?

HENRY: Yes. For the appointments.

CYNTHIA: But I'm not going, Henry.

HENRY: Well, we have the bills. I mean, it's insured, Cynthia, there's very little to pay, but they are here, I know, those bills.

CYNTHIA: I'm sorry, Henry. I didn't realize.

HENRY: It's okay, Cynthia. We'll notify someone.

CYNTHIA: I just thought I should stop.

HENRY: Of course you can stop.

CYNTHIA: Henry, I'm not always sure these people know what they are doing.

HENRY: What people?

CYNTHIA: Well, a doctor.

HENRY: Uh huh, sure. I'm not sure either. I wondered, for example, if he took it personally. The appointments you missed. He seemed, I think, a little stuck on you. At least when he called. I mean, he was very businesslike, there was nothing wrong, I'm sure.

CYNTHIA: I'm sorry, Henry. If he got stuck on me.

HENRY: Well, no. It's not your fault.

CYNTHIA: I just didn't think I should see him anymore.

HENRY: No, sure. Right.
    Well, I'm sure he meant well. These people, generally, mean very well. And it's hard sometimes, I can imagine. Not to get personally involved.

(HENRY *looks blankly at* CYNTHIA's *note. He folds it up.* CYNTHIA *comes to the table.*)

CYNTHIA: Henry. I like your father's painting.

HENRY: Hm?

CYNTHIA: In the front hall. The ocean, I like it.

HENRY: Well, that's fine, Cynthia.

CYNTHIA: You mentioned taking it down. Putting it upstairs. Maybe with Sally.

HENRY: Well, I did mention, yes. But this is fine. It's fine in the hall.

CYNTHIA: You said you felt we had to walk, or step, around it all the time.

HENRY: Cynthia, no, I was in the mood, that's all.
For a change. It might be nice, I thought, to change
the picture in the hall.

CYNTHIA: Yes, but I like it, Henry.

HENRY: Good. So let's keep it. Right where it is.
*(Looks inside the paper bag on the table. He takes out
several refrigerator magnets.)* There're more of these
things. A whole lot more. Sally bought these, you say?

CYNTHIA: Yes.

HENRY: With what? These must have cost ten dollars
apiece.

CYNTHIA: It's pottery, Henry.

HENRY: No, this is porcelain.

CYNTHIA: They can't be ten dollars.

HENRY: Oh, yes, they can.

CYNTHIA: Well, I'm sorry, then. She gave them to me.
They're for me, Henry. She wants me to write notes.

HENRY: Excuse me?

CYNTHIA: Those notes again.

HENRY: What notes?

CYNTHIA: The notes, Henry, I used to write. The
messages for Sally and Chris. So they wouldn't forget
things. Or that I loved them. I left little notes like that.
All over the house. For you too, Henry. Don't you
remember how you used to keep my notes? Well,
there're going to be notes again. That's why Sally
bought all these creatures. To help with the notes.
Get me started. That's all, Henry.

(HENRY takes out more refrigerator magnets.)

HENRY: Uh huh. And how did Sally pay, then?
For these creatures.

CYNTHIA: She charged them.

HENRY: Uh huh?

CYNTHIA: Yes. At the stationery store.

HENRY: What stationery store?

CYNTHIA: Where we get our papers.

HENRY: Oh? She charged them, you say?

CYNTHIA: Well, we charge our papers.

HENRY: Those are newspapers.

CYNTHIA: Henry. Sally's upset.

HENRY: Excuse me?

CYNTHIA: I said, She's upset. She wanted to please me.

HENRY: Cynthia. This is three hundred dollars here.
For knickknacks. I don't know what's more irritating,
Sally's presumption she can charge, or the nerve of
that store.

CYNTHIA: Henry, please. Let's go to breakfast.

HENRY: What?

CYNTHIA: Breakfast, please. You wanted breakfast.
We agreed, Henry.

HENRY: Okay, fine. We'll go to breakfast. *(Puts aside the
paper bag)* I don't know, Cynthia. Sally's never done
anything double minded before. Or sneaky like this.
Her whole life.

CYNTHIA: I know.

HENRY: It's been like a pact between us.
Straightforwardness.

CYNTHIA: She spoke with Ruth.

HENRY: What?

CYNTHIA: Ruth, Henry. She couldn't sleep last night.
Ruth told her you moved your father out of his studio.

HENRY: Ruth told her?

CYNTHIA: Yes. And now she's upset.

HENRY: I didn't move my father out. You know I didn't.
My mother moved him.

CYNTHIA: Ruth feels you helped.

HENRY: What's she talking about? We both had to help.

CYNTHIA: Ruth distorts. I told Sally.

HENRY: Damn.

CYNTHIA: It's all right, Henry. Just talk to Sally. You can
do that. Talk to her.

HENRY: Ruth has a lot of nerve.

CYNTHIA: Henry, we should have said something much
sooner than this.

HENRY: About what?

CYNTHIA: How your father's studio became your
bedroom.

HENRY: Listen. Ruth forgets, years later, how terrified
we were to speak. If we should dare interrupt this
man's thoughts. All his work. Which Ruth decides
now to glorify. A bunch of work which never sold,
never will. Nor did this man do a thing to support his
family. A wife. Who had hopes one day to lift herself
up in this world. None of which Ruth understands
because this man is now an emblem. A symbol
to explain what a raw deal the world is. How her
photographs of dirty laundry and unmade beds,
or crows picking at road kill, are never seen, no.
In a decent gallery. Which is not her fault. No. It's the
world's which also did in her father. And I don't mind
Ruth having these thoughts. Truly. They're hers to

have. But when she starts calling Sally, person-to-person collect, to incite disenchantment with me, or insinuate I should have no say where I send my daughter to school, then I get appalled. And disappointed with Sally, because I thought we agreed. To stop these calls from Ruth. And to stop this constant bickering within herself about where she should go to college. *(Pause)* I'm sorry, Cynthia. You wanted breakfast.

(Pause)

CYNTHIA: Henry. I'm not so sure, myself, anymore.

HENRY: Pardon?

CYNTHIA: About Swarthmore.

HENRY: Oh?

CYNTHIA: Sally's not happy.

HENRY: What?

CYNTHIA: She really doesn't want to stop painting.

HENRY: I'm not asking her to stop.

CYNTHIA: Well, but she thinks you are.

HENRY: That's ridiculous.

CYNTHIA: I don't think so. I think it's become obvious.

HENRY: What's obvious?

CYNTHIA: She doesn't want to go to Swarthmore. It's too close.

HENRY: What's too close?

CYNTHIA: She wants to be further away, Henry, from home.

HENRY: She said that?

CYNTHIA: No, Henry. It's obvious.

(Pause)

HENRY: I'm not sure here, Cynthia. What's obvious.
Maybe what's so obvious are your feelings, that's all.
About Bruce.

CYNTHIA: Bruce?

HENRY: Yes. You'd even encourage her to go to New
York. Or Paris.

CYNTHIA: I don't think I'm encouraging.

HENRY: Bruce is a bargain, Cynthia.

CYNTHIA: I like Bruce.

HENRY: You don't realize it, but he's a bargain.

CYNTHIA: Bruce is fine.

HENRY: Yes, compared to what can happen in New
York. What she'll meet there. Some so-called artist. Or
monkey with painted hair and wind chimes dangling
from his ears. Some barbarian throwback. Born-again
Visigoth, or Pict. Compared to that, yes, Bruce is a
bargain. And on top of which where's Sally, you think,
going to stay? In New York? Where's she going to live?

CYNTHIA: In a dorm?

HENRY: No. She's going to stay at Ruth's.

CYNTHIA: We could tell her not to.

HENRY: Then Ruth would stay with her. And then
the monkey with wind chimes is going to move in,
plus a couple of cats and dogs, then Ruth'll bring a
darkroom into the bathroom, and thousands of lousy
photographs, and where the hell is Sally going to find
anywhere to sit down and study?
Huh? *(Pause)* I'm sorry, Cynthia.
I thought we talked about this. We're already paid for
Swarthmore. *(Pause)* I'm starting to feel lost again. I am.
In my own house. I think certain things have been

decided, put down some place, and I find they haven't
been decided at all. I can't find a thing. I used to know
where things were around here. My green shirt, for
example. I can't find that shirt you bought. People keep
rearranging things. I bump into walls. Chairs fall over.
This never used to happen. It was safer and calm in
here. Focused. Now I find myself in the wrong room,
like the dining room, thinking, why am I here? What
was it I wanted? Or the basement, what am I doing
down here? Or I'll open your closet, even, that's
another thing, I keep going to your closet. Keep
thinking that should be my side of the room. And
I keep asking myself, Cynthia, where's that blue dress
with the clouds, huh? I haven't seen that dress in a long
time. Because that was lovely, Cynthia, it was, when
we went out and bought that dress together.

　　But I'll tell you one thing I do know: it was my mother
who moved my father out of his studio. Not me. My
mother threw the paint brushes out of her kitchen sink.
It was my mother who finally said, Enough. Her
children won't stay like this anymore. Stuck in some
dark corner of a house.

(Pause)

CYNTHIA: Henry. I don't have a blue dress with clouds.

(Pause)

HENRY: You don't?

CYNTHIA: No. I don't.

HENRY: That's not possible.

CYNTHIA: But I don't.

HENRY: That's my favorite dress.

CYNTHIA: Well, I'm sorry.

HENRY: You threw it out?

CYNTHIA: I never had a dress like that.

HENRY: Let's go upstairs. It's in a drawer somewhere, you put it in a drawer, folded it up, I know.

CYNTHIA: Henry, I don't have one.

HENRY: But somewhere.

CYNTHIA: I don't like clouds.

HENRY: Well, not clouds, Cynthia. Wispy things. White splashes, or something. On a dark blue dress.

CYNTHIA: I'm sorry.

HENRY: No, somewhere I've seen you.

CYNTHIA: I never, never had such a dress, Henry. Really. I'm sorry. *(Pause)* Henry?

HENRY: At work, Cynthia, I know exactly where everything is. I swear to you, Cynthia, at work I'm an intelligent man.

CYNTHIA: Henry, what are you doing this morning? After breakfast.

HENRY: I'll, ah, fix the gutter outside. Do the lawn?

CYNTHIA: Would you like to do something else?

HENRY: Better get cracking, huh?

CYNTHIA: Would you like to go shopping?

HENRY: What do we need? Food? We need food?

CYNTHIA: A dress. We need a dress.

HENRY: You want to buy a dress?

CYNTHIA: Well, you buy it. For when I go bowling.

HENRY: Bowling, Cynthia? You hate bowling.

CYNTHIA: I might not. With you and Chris.

HENRY: No, you hate it.

CYNTHIA: No, it might feel different, Henry, in a blue dress. With clouds. Might feel very different, bowling. What do you think?

HENRY: You'd go bowling with us, really?

CYNTHIA: Yes, Henry, I might. In such a dress.

HENRY: You wake up, you know.

CYNTHIA: I could go bowling, I'm sure.

HENRY: Sometimes you really wake up.

CYNTHIA: Yes?

HENRY: Yes. And I find myself waking too. Feel myself wake, Cynthia. From a long slumber.

(HENRY *takes* CYNTHIA's *hand.*)

HENRY: What was it, Cynthia? You used to tell the kids. About a forest. Some story about waking up in a forest?

CYNTHIA: It was nothing, Henry.

HENRY: No, the kids liked it. I remember that.

CYNTHIA: It was just to put them to bed.

HENRY: I don't think so. Sounded more than that. Some story for bed. I mean, there were lots of stories for a while there, actually each night. I remember passing by in the hall. Stopping one time to listen. And there was this girl, or young woman, who had just woken from some terrible battle she was losing, I remember at the very edge, or end, of the world. And she found herself now in a forest. With no idea how she was there, except it was lovely. There were waterfalls and birds. Meadows, I remember. And a wolf, or a bear, that was very friendly. Everything safe and lovely, yes. There was a wizard too. This guy in charge with one eye, like normal, in his head. But his other eye was outside his head, circling, like some tiny moon. And when he

opened his hand you could see the stars he held. A
whole nighttime right there in the palm of his hand.

(Lights focus on HENRY.*)*

HENRY: And I stood there in the door, listening,
thinking, where does she get that from? These ideas?
It sounds so enchanting a story like that. Like she
knows some other world, some invisible, innocent
place right next to here.
   And then I remember the young woman went
exploring one day. With the eye of the wizard. His
eye circled, or orbited, her head instead. And in this
manner they went all the way to the end of the forest.
Where she became afraid. Because she could see trees
disappearing one by one. The ground and the sky too,
vanishing. Melting into a void. So she went back to the
wizard. To tell something dark and silent was eating
away at the edge of his forest. But he said he knew.
Something was coming. And they would have to leave.
Withdraw from the forest. And she asked him, We're
going to withdraw from the forest? And he said, No.
I will take the forest. Take it back again in my head.
And you will help me journey, then. With this forest
I will carry and hold in my thoughts. *(Pause)* And I
thought about that. A wizard carrying a forest in his
head. Going off somewhere safer, I guess, to pitch his
forest. I thought about it as I lay down later in bed.
When all of a sudden one eye left my head and began
to circle me. I couldn't get it to come back. So I got out
of bed to follow after my own eye. Together we went
down the hall and, I thought, out the front door. But
when I looked back, I saw the whole house in my head.
I was walking down hallways, going through doors,
in my own head. And I thought, what land is this?
Where did this land come from in my head?
   And for a moment I felt fear. Utterly unprepared. And
I thought, please, God, don't let me see things like this. I

can't be ready to see like this. Don't make me take this
journey. *(Pause)* When I woke up, the first thing I did
was feel my eyes. I felt them both there. Right in my
head.
  Then I saw the moon outside in the window.
  And I saw my wife fast asleep next to me. And
I watched her, thinking, she's resting now.
  She seems to be resting from some journey, I think.
There's a journey with her. I can't take just now.
With my wife.

(Blackout)

Scene Three

*(The sound of rain. A lights comes up in the front hall.
The kitchen, otherwise, is dark.* CYNTHIA *stands by the
front hall. She turns on a light. She sees* CHRISTOPHER
sitting by himself at the table.)

(It is late that evening.)

*(All the kitchen walls are gone. The rest of the stage beyond is
empty, colorless. The painting from the front hall is sitting in
one of the kitchen chairs. There is a hammer and box of nails
on the table.)*

CYNTHIA: Chris?
  You're sitting by yourself here, Chris. In the dark?
I thought you went to bed.

(No response)

CYNTHIA: I was going to get some ice cream for your
father. Would you like to come in and have some?
We're watching television. *(Sits at the table)* What is it,
Chris?
  Why are you sitting here? In the dark.

*(*CHRISTOPHER *shrugs his shoulders.)*

CYNTHIA: Chris. I worry about you. More than anyone I'm worried about you. You seem more separate. Off by yourself.

CHRISTOPHER: I'm not off by myself. I'm right here in the kitchen.

CYNTHIA: No, Chris. In your thoughts.

CHRISTOPHER: What thoughts?

CYNTHIA: What you think about. Like to imagine.

CHRISTOPHER: I'm separate?

CYNTHIA: Yes. You could become very separate someday. Apart.

CHRISTOPHER: Nah, Mom. That's not going to happen, ever, to me. Getting separated.

CYNTHIA: Okay.

CHRISTOPHER: Yeah, I think you should worry about Sally, Mom. Not me. Yep. Sally's the one gone weird. She used to paint better too. Much better.

CYNTHIA: I don't think so, Chris.

CHRISTOPHER: Hm?

CYNTHIA: I like what Sally paints.

CHRISTOPHER: Oh? You seen it lately?

CYNTHIA: Yes, I have.

CHRISTOPHER: Yeah?

CYNTHIA: I was upstairs. Two weeks ago.

CHRISTOPHER: In Sally's room?

CYNTHIA: Yes. I went up to talk to her. About walking like that outside at night. But she was asleep.

CHRISTOPHER: You saw her painting?

CYNTHIA: Sitting there, yes. In the moonlight.

CHRISTOPHER: The picture of our house?

CYNTHIA: The house?

CHRISTOPHER: Yes, Mom. It's got all the same colors as our house.

CYNTHIA: Well, I liked it, Chris.

CHRISTOPHER: What? You're kidding?

CYNTHIA: No, I did. I liked the woman looking out her window. I liked all the sky about her head. And down below her window sill was empty space. Like a moat, I thought.
    I was pleased. A little amazed. That Sally could paint like that.

(Pause)

CHRISTOPHER: Nah, Mom. You saw it in the moonlight. That's all. Probably that's why you got to like it. 'Cause in the broad daylight, Mom, it's weird. It's nothing at all like what Sally used to do.

(CYNTHIA *takes a box of ice cream out of the refrigerator.*)

CHRISTOPHER: What's happening to Grandpa's painting? Dad going to move it upstairs? Give us something new for the hall?

CYNTHIA: No, Chris. It fell.

CHRISTOPHER: Hm?

CYNTHIA: It fell in the hall there. Your father's nailed the frame back on.

(CHRISTOPHER *regards the painting in the chair.*)

CHRISTOPHER: You know what I was thinking about, Mom? By myself in the dark?

CYNTHIA: What, Chris?

CHRISTOPHER: I was thinking about Ragatelle. How you used to tell us about her. And the wizard who took off. With the forest in his head.

CYNTHIA: Yes?

CHRISTOPHER: I really liked that guy. Always, Mom. The way he had to talk to people. Didn't want anyone to notice all the forest sounds, the birds he could hear, in his head. I thought that was amazing. A whole forest land in his head. How he and Ragatelle could go walk in it. And he was the only one, Mom, who could save her. No knight or warrior champion could do that. Only this skinny-looking wizard.

(HENRY *appears in the front hall.*)

CHRISTOPHER: *(Continuing)* Which I think is cool. How you can never guess sometimes who's going to come and save. Come out of the blue like that. Out of nowhere.
　　I was sitting here, yeah, in the dark thinking, that's what I'd like to learn to do someday. Save people who are in trouble. Come out of the blue like that.

(Pause)

HENRY: Chris?

CHRISTOPHER: *(Turning)* Hm?

HENRY: I thought you went up to bed with Sally.

CHRISTOPHER: I couldn't sleep, Dad.

HENRY: Okay.
　　Would you like to join us, then, for ice cream?

CHRISTOPHER: Nah. I can probably sleep now, thanks.

HENRY: You don't want to stay with us? And talk?

CHRISTOPHER: About what?

HENRY: I don't know. Wizards, maybe. Or how you'll be in the movies someday.

CHRISTOPHER: Nah. I'd rather get some sleep.

HENRY: I understand.

CHRISTOPHER: Fine, guys.

CYNTHIA: Goodnight, Chris.

CHRISTOPHER: Okay, Mom. Goodnight, guys. *(Exits)*

HENRY: Everything all right?

CYNTHIA: Yes, Henry.

HENRY: You didn't get the ice cream.

CYNTHIA: No, I'm sorry.

HENRY: Should I get it?

CYNTHIA: Yes, would you? I'll go inside. Watch the news.

HENRY: Sure.

CYNTHIA: Not too much, Henry.

HENRY: Too much?

CYNTHIA: Ice cream.

HENRY: Right.

(CYNTHIA picks up the painting in the chair.)

CYNTHIA: I'm going to put this back, Henry. Thank you.

HENRY: Hm?

CYNTHIA: For fixing the painting. I'll put it in the hall.

HENRY: Good.

(Exit CYNTHIA. HENRY regards the box of ice cream. He brings out two bowls. He opens a drawer and gets two spoons. He continues to look through the drawer. Enter SALLY from the lawn outside)

HENRY: Oh. Where have you been?

SALLY: Outside.

HENRY: Doing what?

SALLY: Just outside.

HENRY: Outside. Okay. *(Opens another drawer. He looks through it.)*

HENRY: I thought you went to bed. I thought everybody went to bed.

SALLY: I woke up.

HENRY: I'm sorry. Something wrong?

SALLY: Nope. Just didn't sleep.

(HENRY goes to the dishwasher. He looks inside.)

HENRY: Stopped raining, huh?

SALLY: Uh huh.

HENRY: Would you like some ice cream?

SALLY: No, thank you.

HENRY: We're having ice cream. *(Opens closets. He looks through them.)* Sally, where's the scooper? I can't find the scooper.

SALLY: I don't know.

HENRY: Did you use the scooper last?

SALLY: No.

HENRY: Did Christopher?

SALLY: I don't know.

HENRY: Sally. Could you help me a little with this, I can't find the scooper.

SALLY: You could use a spoon.

HENRY: Okay, I could use a spoon, but the scooper's got to be here somewhere.

(SALLY *looks through drawers.*)

HENRY: I don't know, the last time I saw it was last night. Sally, I looked there.

SALLY: You could have missed it.

HENRY: But I looked there.

SALLY: When I'm looking for something I often find it right where I looked first. (*Opens the dishwasher*)

HENRY: I looked there too. You saw me look.

SALLY: Okay. Where do you want me to look?

HENRY: There are plenty of places.

(SALLY *opens the refrigerator.*)

HENRY: Ah, now. Sally.

SALLY: Christopher could have left it here. This is where he eats.

HENRY: Did Christopher have ice cream?

SALLY: I don't know.

HENRY: We've got to find that scooper.

(SALLY *slams drawers and objects on the counters, looking for the scooper.* HENRY *turns and watches her.*)

HENRY: Ah, Sally? What's that under your raincoat?

SALLY: I'm looking, Dad, I'm looking.

HENRY: No, wait. Hold on, Sally.

SALLY: I'm looking.

HENRY: Sally, stop!

SALLY: You found the scooper?

HENRY: Where'd you get that dress, Sally? That's your mother's dress.

SALLY: This isn't Mom's dress.

HENRY: Yes, it is. We tried to find one just like that today.

SALLY: You gave me this dress, Dad.

HENRY: Sally. I did not give you a dress like that.

SALLY: Yes, you did, did you forget when you gave me this dress!?

HENRY: Sally, don't take that tone, all right?

SALLY: Did you forget?

HENRY: Sally, I know that's your mother's dress.

SALLY: It is not!

HENRY: Come on, Sally, hey, quiet.

SALLY: You can ask Mom.

HENRY: When? When did I give it to you?

SALLY: Last summer.

HENRY: I did, huh? Last summer, what for?

SALLY: If you don't remember, that's your problem. This is my dress.

HENRY: Sally. If you want to be rude about this, then just go upstairs, kindly take that dress off, and put it back in your mother's closet.

(Pause)

SALLY: Okay. I'll go upstairs. And put it in Mom's closet. (Starts to exit)

HENRY: Sally?

SALLY: What?

HENRY: Did I give you that dress? A blue dress like that? With clouds. Wispy white things.

SALLY: Yes.

HENRY: For any particular reason? Or just because we saw it somewhere?

SALLY: We went out to buy a dress.

HENRY: But I don't usually buy dresses for you. Your mother does that.

SALLY: You bought it for me.

HENRY: Sally, I don't remember.

(Pause)

SALLY: Remember, Dad, don't you remember when I was working in the restaurant last summer? I came home one night, real upset, and I wouldn't tell you. And you kept asking, until I told you the restaurant owner was bothering me.

HENRY: Oh, yes, sure. I remember that.

SALLY: You told me to quit. Then one night when it was really crowded, you went into that restaurant. And in front of all the customers, started shouting and hollering at the owner about what a dirty old man he was.

HENRY: Oh, boy. Yes.

SALLY: That's when you gave me this dress. The next day.

HENRY: Yes. Yes, okay.

SALLY: You said, Let's go out and celebrate and buy you a dress.

HENRY: Just you and me.

SALLY: That's right.

HENRY: Yes, I remember.

SALLY: I really liked you that day.

HENRY: Yes, it was a good day. It was fun.

SALLY: Really liked you sitting in the store, watching me model almost thirty dresses.

HENRY: A lot of dresses, yes. That was nice, yes. Really. That poor restaurant. Boy, that was something.

(*Pause*)

SALLY: You forgot?

HENRY: Yes, I'm sorry. I'm sorry, I don't know how I could forget.

SALLY: It's okay.

HENRY: Sally, when you get older, umm, at least for me as I get older, things get jumbled a bit in my mind. It's hard to stay focused. At home. At work, I'm fine. But here I'm a little lost. I don't know too much about what goes on around here.
   We never found that scooper.
   I'm sorry. I forgot. (*He takes a spoon. He uses the spoon to put ice cream into the bowls.*) Looks nice, Sally. That dress. Very nice still. Decided to try it on again, huh?
   Wish I knew where that scooper was.
   Sally, Mom told me this morning you don't want to go to college around here. You still want New York. I told her I don't know what your situation with Bruce is, but I thought we did agree. A broader background, a degree in something wider, a liberal arts degree, you know, might serve you better in the long run. Didn't we agree to all this?
   Sure would be easier with a scooper.
   Didn't we? And didn't we also agree about Ruth? These conversations with my sister?

Damn. I wish I knew where it was. I can't find a damn thing in this house. Ever.

SALLY: Does it take as long to find the scooper in your other house?

HENRY: Does it take as long?

SALLY: Yes.

HENRY: No?

SALLY: That's good.

HENRY: What are you talking about, Sally?

SALLY: Your other house.

HENRY: What other house?

SALLY: Your house, Dad. The one you went to visit.

(Pause)

HENRY: I don't know what you're talking about, Sally. *(Puts the ice cream away in the refrigerator)* Well, listen, Sally. When you're ready, we should really talk about this college business, get it settled once again, because as far as I know it's too late to get registered at another college.

SALLY: It's not too late.

HENRY: Well, if you want to be non-matriculated or something.

SALLY: I'm going to New York.

HENRY: Oh?

SALLY: I'm going to try out different schools in New York.

HENRY: You're going to try out different schools? What's that mean?

SALLY: I'll try Parsons, Visual Arts, Pratt, a couple of others. Take a course at each.

HENRY: Oh?

SALLY: And I'm going to stay at Ruth's.

HENRY: You're going to stay with Ruth?

SALLY: That's right.

HENRY: Young lady.

SALLY: Yes?

HENRY: Young lady, even assuming I send you to New York, you're not going to stay with Ruth. You're going to stay in a dorm. And you're not going to bounce from school to school.

SALLY: Yes, I am, Dad. Just like Grandpa.

HENRY: What?

SALLY: I don't want to stay in a dorm. How can I stay in a dorm? If you want to paint you have to try out different schools. Different teachers. Like Grandpa did.

HENRY: Your grandfather has nothing to do with this.

SALLY: Yes, he does, Dad.

HENRY: Sally.

SALLY: You don't understand that, do you?

HENRY: Understand what?

SALLY: Do you? Grandpa just shouldn't have had a family, that's all.

HENRY: What?

SALLY: He could have been a painter. Your father could have been a great painter and you didn't even understand that!

(Pause)

HENRY: What are you, Sally? Some kind of apparition. A bunch of phantom notions come from the past. A

visitation, are you, from my own father? Is this what's
been lurking all along? In my own house? This is what
nips, now, at my heels? Distracts my focus?
  I don't know what you and Ruth have talked about.
Deep in the night. But Ruth has a lot of nerve.

SALLY: No, she doesn't, Dad.

HENRY: Sally, I understand my father wanted to paint.
I've spent my whole life understanding. And if he
hadn't had a family, Sally, like you suggest, where do
you think, then, we would be? You and I, right now,
huh? What world, Sally? What world would there
be for us? If this man had truly gone and painted.

SALLY: What world, Dad?

HENRY: Yes. And who do you think supports your
grandmother now? Who takes care of the whole mess
your grandfather left behind? Has Ruth told you that?
Who fills in for your grandfather now?

SALLY: You, I suppose.

HENRY: You suppose?

SALLY: Yes.

HENRY: Just like that, you suppose?

SALLY: Yes, Dad.

HENRY: Sally, you know nothing about living in a tiny
house. A cramped, dirty place. Like a cave. With two
parents arguing. Dragging us all down to this day.
You know nothing how bleak, and dark, and hopeless a
place it is your father had to come from. Nothing about
what it took to get this other house. Where we live.
What kind of work. What thorough kind of thinking.
  No, instead, you suppose. You suppose any damn
thing you please.
  Well. Let's just get our supposes straight, little lady.
Which is you are entirely free to paint and to educate

yourself to paint. I have worked hard to provide you with that freedom, and I will continue to provide. But you will not commandeer me into sending you to New York without so much as a by-your-leave.

(Pause)

SALLY: *(quietly)* Did you ask for leave?

HENRY: What?

SALLY: You didn't ask for leave. You didn't ask Mom's leave. You didn't ask me or anybody. For leave.

(Pause)

HENRY: You're not staying at Ruth's, Sally.

SALLY: Yes, I am, Dad.

(Pause)

HENRY: Would you like some ice cream?

SALLY: No.

HENRY: Have some ice cream.

SALLY: I don't want any ice cream.

HENRY: That upset, huh?

SALLY: Yes.

HENRY: Have some ice cream, anyway.

SALLY: No, Dad. Keep away.

HENRY: No, it'll help you sleep.

SALLY: Stay away from me, Dad.

(Pause)

HENRY: I thought we were friends.
    No, Sally, we were. I used to give you advice. You always asked if you looked okay. Before you went out. You used to tell me what bothered you. I could take care of it. Like the restaurant. *(Pause)* I didn't ever think.

This could become real.
This was just a phase. I thought. *(Pause)* There it is.
The scooper. Somebody left it on top of the refrigerator.

(Enter CYNTHIA*)*

CYNTHIA: Henry?

HENRY: Hm?

CYNTHIA: Henry, what's taking you so long?

HENRY: I'm talking to Sally.

CYNTHIA: I don't think I want any ice cream, Henry.

HENRY: Oh, but I got it already.

CYNTHIA: It's all soft.

HENRY: We've been talking.

CYNTHIA: I'll go to bed now, I think.

HENRY: You don't want your ice cream?

CYNTHIA: No, you put it away.

HENRY: Well, all right.

SALLY: You have a headache, Mom?

CYNTHIA: No, just tired.

HENRY: Well, that's okay, you go on up to bed.
I'll be up in a while.

CYNTHIA: What were you talking about?

SALLY: College.

CYNTHIA: Oh? Perhaps I should join you.

SALLY: No, you're tired.

CYNTHIA: No, maybe I should.

SALLY: This is between Dad and me.

CYNTHIA: Oh?

SALLY: Besides, you needn't worry because I'm going to New York.

CYNTHIA: You are?

SALLY: This is what Dad and I are discussing right now. We just have to work out a couple of details, but I'm going to New York.

CYNTHIA: What kind of details?

SALLY: Well, we're working them out. It's between the two of us. We'll let you know.

CYNTHIA: I don't quite understand.

SALLY: It's all right, Mom. Dad and I are having a problem about where I'm going to stay in New York, because I'm going to be staying at Ruth's.

CYNTHIA: Henry, is she going to Ruth's?

SALLY: Mom, Dad and I have to talk because Ruth is his sister, and he thinks he knows a lot of stuff about her, but she's also my friend. So it's between us. *(Pause)* We're not going to be long, Mom. You'll see Dad soon.

CYNTHIA: Goodnight, then, Sally.

SALLY: Goodnight, Mom.

HENRY: Ah, Cynthia.

CYNTHIA: Henry?

HENRY: Just a minute, please.
   Sally?
   Sally, I make a living getting out of the armlocks people think they have me in. I do it all the time, little lady, every day, all day, and that's why we live here. In the style that we are living. And you obviously have not dealt with me in any business context. But you've visited me at work. Seen me do it, as much as you could understand it, and furthermore the few times you've tried to browbeat me, it's never worked, has it now?

(No response)

HENRY: Little lady. If you feel so impelled, you are at perfect liberty to tell your mother you saw me spending time with another woman. *(Pause)* Cynthia. Sally would like you to know that I went to bed last night with someone else.

CYNTHIA: Yes?

HENRY: Yes.

CYNTHIA: Sally wants me to know?

HENRY: Yes. *(Pause)* Meanwhile, our arrangement, Sally, while I'm paying your bills, in particular the bills for college, is that you will comply with what I see fit. You are free, obviously, to try to change my mind, but twisting my arm is not a good idea. Is that understood?

CYNTHIA: Did you want me to know, Henry?

(Pause)

HENRY: Sally, I'd appreciate it now if you'd get your tailend up to bed. And leave me alone with your mother.

(SALLY starts to exit.)

CYNTHIA: Sally?

SALLY: Mom?

CYNTHIA: Sally. It's all right.

SALLY: Yes?

CYNTHIA: Don't be afraid.

SALLY: Mom, I'm sorry.

CYNTHIA: It's all right.

SALLY: Mom, I didn't mean anything.

CYNTHIA: Sally?

SALLY: I didn't.

CYNTHIA: Sally, remember last winter when you found me crying on the stairs?

SALLY: Yes?

CYNTHIA: Remember we went walking in the snow?

SALLY: Yes. We went through a couple of fields together.

CYNTHIA: That's it.

SALLY: Nobody'd walked on the snow yet.

CYNTHIA: Yes, we were closest I felt in a long time. Talking about school.

SALLY: And painting.

CYNTHIA: Yes. We did a lot of talking.

SALLY: For the first time, uh huh. Since the hospital.

CYNTHIA: Yes, thank you. Because I never thought to spend that time with you. I didn't.

SALLY: No, I know. You were on the stairs.

CYNTHIA: I thought I should spend it with Doctor Heisel. Yes, that's who I thought I should spend the first day of snow with.

SALLY: Yes?

CYNTHIA: Because I would go into that office. And talk about snow.

SALLY: Okay, Mom.

CYNTHIA: It's what we talked about, this man and I. The first day of snow, when it would snow. We both liked snow. I was keeping him away, putting it off, until it snowed, at least till then. And then it would pass, I thought, these feelings have to pass. But then it did snow. On a Saturday. I was in the living room when I saw it. And I turned from the window. Went

for the phone in here, to call. Tell him, Quick. Look out
the window. But you were here, right here next to the
phone, eating. So without thinking I started up the
stairs for the other phone. But halfway up, I heard your
father upstairs. And I stopped, thinking, it's Saturday.
That's what it is. It's snowing now on a Saturday.
  And then it smacked me right in the chest. It's
Saturday. And I sat down on the steps, halfway up,
not breathing, thinking, I'm not breathing. No. At all.
And it stayed there, sitting on my chest, leaning there,
this deadness, I'm tired, it's Saturday, I can't be living,
can't feel this way any longer.
  And all of a sudden, I cried. I started to cry. And Sally
heard me. Came up the stairs to me.

SALLY: Mom?

CYNTHIA: And I couldn't tell her anything. Except it
was snowing.

SALLY: Mom?

CYNTHIA: And that made me cry more.

SALLY: Dad?

CYNTHIA: But I was breathing. And while I was
breathing, I got up and quick asked Sally to come
take a walk with me.

SALLY: Dad, Mom's gone funny.

CYNTHIA: In the snow. I asked her. Come walk in the
snow with me.

(HENRY *comes forward. He takes* CYNTHIA'*s hand.*)

CYNTHIA: Can we? Can we do that? Please?

HENRY: Yes, Cynthia. We'll do that.

CYNTHIA: We'll do that? We'll put our boots on and
take a walk?

HENRY: In the snow. That's right.

(Pause)

CYNTHIA: Henry, there's that dress. Remember?
That dress on Sally.

HENRY: Yes, Cynthia.

CYNTHIA: The one I wanted to go bowling in.
Remember?

HENRY: I remember, yes.

(CYNTHIA steps away from HENRY. She reaches out for SALLY. The stage darkens. A lights focuses on CYNTHIA.)

CYNTHIA: *(Still reaching)* Sally? *(She reaches out into the darkness. Turning)* Chris?

(No response)

CYNTHIA: Please, God. Don't let my head explode.
Please, God. If I should take this journey.

(Blackout)

Scene Four

(The kitchen. All the walls, cabinets, appliances are gone. What is left are the table and four chairs.)

(A sheet hangs in the air where the refrigerator was. On the sheet is written in large letters: "Sally's gone, she left her name.")

(The stage beyond is empty, colorless.)

(HENRY and SALLY sit at the table. It is the next morning.)

SALLY: Dad?

HENRY: Hm?

SALLY: Dad, you want breakfast?

HENRY: No.

SALLY: I can make breakfast.

HENRY: Thanks, no.

SALLY: Something else?

HENRY: Hm?

SALLY: A glass of juice?

HENRY: Nothing, Sally. Really.

(Pause)

SALLY: Should I take the sheet down? The sheet, Dad?

(No response)

(CHRISTOPHER appears. He walks across the stage. He comes to the table.)

HENRY: Christopher.

CHRISTOPHER: Hi, guys.

SALLY: Hello, Christopher.

(CHRISTOPHER sees the sheet. Pause)

CHRISTOPHER: *(Reading)* "Sally's gone, she left her name." *(Pause)* Dad. How come you're letting Sally ruin a good sheet like that?

HENRY: Sally didn't write that.

CHRISTOPHER: No?

HENRY: Your mother did.

(Pause)

CHRISTOPHER: Uh huh. Somebody got something to tell me around here?
   Where's Mom?

HENRY: Your mother left.

CHRISTOPHER: She did?

HENRY: She packed a bag and left.

CHRISTOPHER: Where's she going?

HENRY: We don't know.

CHRISTOPHER: She didn't tell you?

HENRY: No. She got up in the middle of the night and left.

CHRISTOPHER: Why?

HENRY: Because Sally and I had an argument in front of her after you went to bed. She found out that Bruce and Sally saw me with another woman.

CHRISTOPHER: Oh. *(Pause)* Okay. *(Pause)* What'd she write this for?

HENRY: I'm not sure.

CHRISTOPHER: Kind of crazy to write Sally.

HENRY: I think so.

CHRISTOPHER: Unless Mom thinks Sally has something to do with this.

HENRY: Such as, Chris?

CHRISTOPHER: Yeah, well. Did you call anybody?

HENRY: Doctor Heisel.

CHRISTOPHER: Yeah?

HENRY: He doesn't know where she is.

CHRISTOPHER: She could be hiding there anyway.

HENRY: We looked.

SALLY: We looked lots of places, Chris.

CHRISTOPHER: Well, I don't know. I get up this morning and find out I wasn't consulted about whether we have a mom here or not.

HENRY: There was no consulting.

CHRISTOPHER: Yeah, okay. It seems to me you guys screwed up. *(Pause)* Didn't you?

HENRY: That's right.

(CHRISTOPHER turns from HENRY.)

CHRISTOPHER: You really screwed it, didn't you, Sally? Couldn't stay out of it, could you? I mean, I don't think it's any of our business what Mom and Dad do in their spare time. Just like they got to stay out of my spare time. I mean, as long as nobody gets nasty about it, I don't know, it's probably all right. But you had to step in, didn't you, Sally? Huh?
  Didn't you?
  And that's because you're jealous. You're jealous 'cause Mom's smarter and prettier and more quiet than you'll ever be, and you're jealous too Mom's got Dad, but as soon as Dad went and got anybody else, as soon as Dad went through some phase, you couldn't stand it! You had to blurt it all out!

HENRY: Christopher.

CHRISTOPHER: You had to mess up our whole family!

HENRY: Christopher, lay off Sally, all right!

CHRISTOPHER: Sure, I'll lay off Sally. I'll just knock her face off when you're not around.

HENRY: No, you won't, Christopher.

CHRISTOPHER: Sure, I will.

HENRY: What's the matter with you, don't you have guts?

CHRISTOPHER: Sure, I have guts.

HENRY: Then what the hell are you picking on Sally for?

(Pause)

CHRISTOPHER: You used to tell a story, Dad. The one story I remember you told. How Mom came from the next life we were supposed to live. Where people were better. Took care of each other. You said our family was lucky. Cause there'd been a mistake, and Mom was with us instead. And you told me if you ever took your eyes off Mom, you'd turn around and she'd be gone. You wouldn't know how. She could have just crumpled up, right in the air, and slipped away. That's why you married Mom. It's best way you could figure to keep your eyes on her. And I used to ask you, Can I help? Can I help, Dad? And you said, Sure. I could help. I could watch Mom too. *(Pause)* If you tell something like that, to a little kid, I was a little kid, you got to make it real. Otherwise you have no business telling it.

SALLY: But Dad believed it was true, Chris.

(Pause)

HENRY: Christopher, would you like to come with me? Please?

CHRISTOPHER: Where?

HENRY: Into town.

CHRISTOPHER: What for?

HENRY: You and I could do some shopping.

CHRISTOPHER: I don't like shopping.

SALLY: I'll go, Dad.

HENRY: You sure, Chris? We could look for Mom.

CHRISTOPHER: I HATE SHOPPING!

(Pause)

HENRY: I wanted to go with you, Christopher. That's all.
    I've spent most of my life. Almost all my life, Chris.
Repairing what I thought your grandfather did to me.
    I thought I might talk with you.

Because if you. Either of you, Sally. Spends your time, the way I have, counteracting what I have done to you, then I'm sorry. And we must do something. Do something, don't you think? Together about this? *(Pause)* I'll leave you alone, then?

SALLY: Okay.

HENRY: You want something special?

SALLY: Nothing, no.

HENRY: If your mother calls, tell her I'm looking. I'm out there looking. I'll be right back, okay?

SALLY: I'll talk to her, Dad. I will.

HENRY: Good. Good, keep her on the phone.

SALLY: Chris, okay?

HENRY: That would be nice. Thanks, Sally. *(Exits)*

(Pause)

SALLY: You want something to eat?

CHRISTOPHER: I don't want breakfast.

SALLY: You want sandwiches?

(No response)

(SALLY looks behind the hanging sheet. The stage beyond begins to take on color.)

SALLY: There's no cheese, Chris.

CHRISTOPHER: Hm?

SALLY: I'm sorry. You must have eaten all the cheese.

CHRISTOPHER: How about spaghetti cheese?

SALLY: Hm?

CHRISTOPHER: Bring some, okay? Cheese for spaghetti.

(SALLY *takes the sheet down.* CHRISTOPHER *sits at the table making a sandwich. An ocean beach begins to take up the whole stage beyond.*)

CHRISTOPHER: I think I'm going to be a movie star. I think that's the only thing left for me to do.

SALLY: Hm?

CHRISTOPHER: Don't you want to be a movie star?

SALLY: How come?

CHRISTOPHER: I think if you're a movie star you can make better sense out of everything.

SALLY: Christopher.

CHRISTOPHER: I like spaghetti cheese.

SALLY: That's a sandwich.

CHRISTOPHER: You said there's no cheese.

SALLY: It's for spaghetti, Chris.

CHRISTOPHER: I like it.

SALLY: Gross.

CHRISTOPHER: I like lonesome girls too.

SALLY: What?

CHRISTOPHER: You look lonesome. A lonesome girl.

SALLY: Christopher, stop playing.

CHRISTOPHER: No, I do.

SALLY: Stop smiling like a movie star.

CHRISTOPHER: Who, me?

SALLY: You're always pretending.

CHRISTOPHER: You got something better to do?

(CHRISTOPHER *turns away from* SALLY. *He continues to eat. The sound of the ocean*)

SALLY: Chris?

(No response)

SALLY: Chris, I pretend too. Talk to myself. All the time,
I do, in my head. You should hear the things I have to
say. Stuff I say to you. In particular, you. Corny stuff,
even.
   Chris, I say things in my head, hopes, stuff like that,
that sound just awful when I say them out loud. I've
tried it. Doesn't sound at all like it did when I just
thought it. It's the same with everybody. The same,
I bet. 'Cause there's some kind of background music
inside your head.

(The sound of the ocean continues.)

SALLY: I don't mean there's music, but something.
Because if I say in my head, for example, I love you,
Christopher, there's a background music. Otherwise
how could I say it? And I can get goosebumps on my
arms from thinking about you, Christopher. I can. But
if I actually said to you, I love you, Christopher. Or if
I said, I'm sorry. I'm sorry I made what happened to
Mom. I never meant what happened to Mom. I don't
know how I could have ever got so angry. To make
what happened like that to Mom.

(Pause. CHRISTOPHER is gone.)

SALLY: If I said that, immediately I would feel phony.
And you too. 'Cause something's awkward. And we'd
have to argue right away to get back to normal. And I
don't understand how come. How come the longer you
stay in this world, the longer you see everything going
on, the harder and harder it gets to say what you mean.
Or why you have to keep it all in your head. The older
you get, the more and more stuff you have to keep
in your head. Any kind of hopes you ever had about
living, all of it, never speaking, and it gets sicker and
sicker inside your head, until you can't hold it up

anymore, and you're ashamed, and you fall over, get old, and die. *(Pause)* I love you, Christopher. *(Pause)* I love Dad, too. *(Pause)* Mom. *(Pause)* I love you, Mom. From as far away as you have to get from me.

(The ocean continues. Blackout)

END OF PLAY

www.ingramcontent.com/pod-product-compliance
Lightning Source LLC
Chambersburg PA
CBHW052150090426
42741CB00010B/2213